BUDDHISM

A new approach

Steve Clarke & Mel Thompson

290/CLA

Hodder & Stoughton
MEMBER OF THE HODDER HEADLINE GROUP

Acknowledgements

The Publishers would like to thank the following for permission to reproduce copyright illustrations in this volume:

Steve Clarke p52; ClearVision p51(top), 85; Dharmacharini Khemasiddhi p123; Philip Emmett p11, 15, 19, 35, 41, 55, 65, 75, 81, 86, 95, 112(bottom), 113, 114; Japanese National Tourist Office p43, 49; NASA p20; David Rose p5, 10, 79, 83, 84, 87, 89, 94, 98, 99(bottom), 105, 110 (left), 116; Valerie Simpson p17, 39; Mel Thompson p 45, 46, 50, 51(bottom), 53, 73, 99(top), 110(right), 112(top), 120, 124.

The Publishers would also like to thank Beacon Press for permission to reproduce an extract from 'Dhyana for Beginners' in the translation given in *A Buddhist Bible* by Dwight Goddard.

British Library Cataloguing in Publication Data
Clarke, Steve and Thompson, Mel
Buddhism: New Approach
I. Title II. Thompson, M. R.
294.3

ISBN 0 340 63922 9

First published 1996
Impression number 10 9 8 7 6 5 4 3 2 1
Year 1999 1998 1997 1996

Printed for Hodder & Stoughton Educational, a division of Hodder Headline Plc, 338 Euston Road, London NW1 3BH by Colorcraft Ltd, Hong Kong

The Cover Illustration

The illustration on the cover is of a lotus flower. Lotuses grow up out of the mud and through the water until, when conditions are just right, they emerge into the air and open to display their beauty. The lotus is therefore a symbol of the Buddhist path towards enlightenment.

This book, although offering a factual account of the Buddhist religion, also seeks to encourage reflection on those qualities of compassion and insight that may lead to the flowering of each individual.

The artwork in this book is by

Dharmachari Aloka

a member of the Western Buddhist Order.

Contents

Introduction

Buddhism is a path that seeks to lead individuals from a life constricted by greed, hatred and ignorance, to one liberated by generosity, compassion and insight. Its aim is to overcome suffering and to promote happiness.

Although Buddhism is called a religion, it is radically different from the other major world religions. It requires no belief in God, but simply a willingness to commit oneself to following the Buddha (the ideal of enlightenment), the Dharma (his teaching) and the Sangha (the community of his followers). Nor does it require blind faith or conformity; each person is expected to examine and test out the teaching and to follow the path in his or her own particular way.

On a personal level, Buddhism is also about being awake, being alert and taking responsibility for your life:

Being awake - because Buddhists believe that everyone has the potential to become enlightened, to be fully awake to the reality of life.

Being alert - because Buddhists seek to avoid those things which dull the mind and to develop their awareness of themselves, their feelings and the world around them.

Taking responsibility for your life - because Buddhists believe that life is always changing, and that people have the ability to respond to it creatively.

This book will introduce you to the main teachings and practices of the Buddhist path. It does not seek to convert you to Buddhism, but simply invites you to consider the Buddha's teachings, and to reflect on your own life in the light of them.

A note for teachers

The 'new approach' series of textbooks seeks to offer the core of factual information required for GCSE examinations, but to do so in the context of the broader aims of religious education at Key Stage 4 and above. It therefore attempts to present a balance between the factual and the experiential approaches to religion.

This balance reflects the conviction that one can only understand a religion once one has allowed its teachings, at least to some extent, to inform and challenge one's own view of life. Equally, a personal quest for insight and meaning cannot but benefit from an examination of the teachings of the world's great religions.

Buddhist terms may appear in either Pali or Sanskrit:
Pali words are marked (P)
Sanskrit words are marked (Sk)

1

The Buddha

- The World into which Siddhartha was Born
- How do we Know about Siddhartha?
- His Birth and Early Life
- His Religious Quest
- Enlightenment
- Teaching
- The Death of the Buddha
- Other Buddhas

Buddhists follow the teaching and example of Siddhartha Gautama, a man who lived in the 6th century BCE in Northern India. They believe that he became 'enlightened', in other words, that he came to understand the truth about life. Buddhists believe that everyone has the potential to become enlightened and that, by practising their religion, they will develop wisdom and happiness.

Within Buddhism there are other Buddhas, and in some traditions everyone is said to have a Buddha-nature within himself or herself. In this chapter, however, we shall be concerned only with the life of Siddhartha.

Buddhists do not think of the Buddha as a god, but as an enlightened human being. He inspired people by what he did and what he taught, so that they followed him and tried to put his teachings into practice.

The title 'Buddha' means 'one who is enlightened', or 'fully awake'. Buddhists contrast this with the unenlightened state in which a person has a view of the world which is distorted by the 'three poisons' of greed, hatred and ignorance.

The World into which Siddhartha was Born

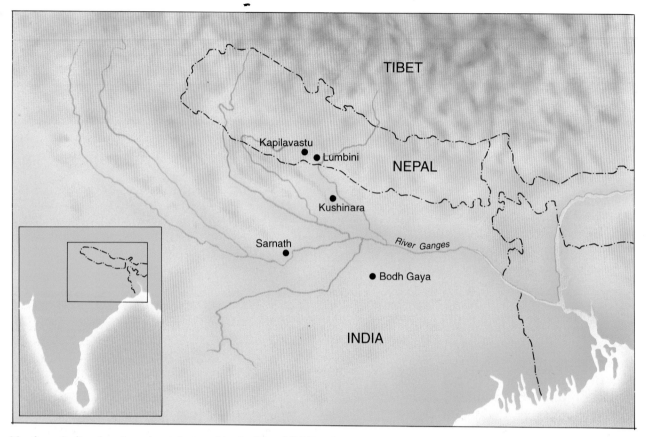

Northern India: showing places featured in the life of Siddhartha.

Siddhartha Gautama lived in Northern India, and spent most of his life teaching in the cities of the Ganges plain. The usual dates given for his life are from 563 to 483BCE, although some modern scholars have suggested that he might have lived about a century later.

At that time, large parts of the Ganges plain were still forested, but there were substantial towns and cities as well as small agricultural villages. The area was fertile and life seems to have been reasonable for most of the people. There is no mention in the Buddhist scriptures of widespread hardship or famine. The cities were able to support a wealthy class of merchants and traders and there were priests and other religious teachers. Although Siddhartha originally went out to a forested place to meditate and seek spiritual guidance, the Buddha did much of his teaching in these cities, and was known to and supported by many wealthy people.

The organised religion of that time was what we now call 'Hindu'. But then, as now, there was no single Hindu religion, just a great variety of Indian religious traditions and practices.

Society was divided up by the caste system. The Brahmin (priestly) class had a strong influence on the formal religion of the day. But they were not the only source of religious ideas, for there were wandering, freelance religious teachers, each of whom would attract a number of followers, by whom they would be supported. They would travel from place to place teaching, and people would offer them food in order to allow them to continue their work. They were not thought of as 'begging', for supporting religious people in this way was an accepted part of Indian society. When the Buddha became enlightened and started to travel around preaching, he was seen as one of a large number of such wandering preachers. They were generally called 'Sadhus' or 'Shramanas'.

The highest caste were the Brahmins (priests)

next came the Kshatriyas (traditionally soldiers and civil servants)

then the Vaishyas (merchants)

and finally the Shudras (manual workers)

Below these four general castes were the 'outcastes', who took the most menial jobs and were separated from the higher castes.

Activity and discussion
Although the caste system does not exist in the West, some jobs have greater status than others. Write a list of ten jobs and put them in order of status. Do you think this is a good or a bad thing? What would happen if they all had the same status?

There was a mixture of the formal religion, based on the Hindu Vedas (scriptures) and controlled by the Brahmin cast, and that of the more informal and varied religious teachers. In general, it seems to have been a time when people were asking religious questions, and willing to explore new ideas. Perhaps this was partly because it was a time of social change. Many people were moving into cities, breaking connections with their village communities.

The Ganges plain in the sixth and fifth centuries BCE was therefore very different from the present day, either in India or in the West. But that does not mean that it was in any sense primitive. The break up of rural life, the pressures of business and city life and the freedom to challenge established ideas and traditions were as real to the people then as they are today.

Activities

Key Elements

1 Where did the Buddha live?
2 What does 'enlightenment' mean?

3 What are the Three Poisons?
4 What were wandering preachers called?

Think about it

5 Find out what 'inspire' means. How does the literal meaning of this word relate to religion?
6 Do you have a hero? Someone who inspires you? Someone whom you would like to follow or be like? List the qualities you would expect to find in such a person.
7 Why do you think Brahmins (priests) were at the 'top' of the caste system?

8 Why did people explore new ideas in India in 6th and 5th centuries BCE?
9 Individual people are influenced by the society in which they life. Do you think it would have been easier or more difficult to be religious if you lived in India at the time of the Buddha compared with life today? Give your reasons.

How do we Know about Siddhartha?

For about 600 years, stories about the Buddha were passed on by word of mouth. They were told in order to illustrate his teachings and inspire his followers. (Most of the Buddha's teachings were written down between 100 BCE and 400 CE and until then, like the stories about his life, they were passed down by word of mouth.) The earliest written account of his life is Ashvagosha's *Buddha Carita* (Works of the Buddha) which comes from about 100CE.

Because they were told for religious reasons, the stories about the Buddha have religious significance and may not all be historical fact. Some of the traditions about the Buddha have been elaborated into religious myths, as is usual with stories of great religious leaders. They express the devotion of his followers. We do know, however, that the Buddha spent about forty five years travelling and teaching in Northern India, dealing with people's individual problems, developing his teachings and spiritual practices to suit the people he met and organising his followers, many of whom became wandering teachers like himself.

> ## Discussion
> Does it matter that the stories of the Buddha were written down so long after his death?

His Birth and Early Life

Siddhartha Gautama was born in a place called Lumbini, in the foothills of the Himalayas. The place is marked by a stone pillar, erected by the Emperor Asoka in the third century BCE, simply stating 'Here was born Shakyamuni.' (Shakyamuni is a title given to Siddhartha. It means 'wise man of the Shakyas' - because Siddhartha was born into the Shakya clan.

Siddhartha is described as a prince, living in a palace, but this does not mean that he would have ruled over a wide area, for much of that part of India was controlled by tribal groups which were governed by communities of elders drawn from the leading families. Siddhartha was born into one of those ruling families. At that time there were also two major kingdoms - Magadha and Kosala - and in his adult life the Buddha was a friend of both of their kings.

In the story of Siddhartha's birth, Queen Maya, wife of Raja Shuddhodana of the Kingdom of Kapilavastu, dreamed that an elephant with six tusks and a head the colour of rubies came down from highest heaven to enter her womb through her right side. Eight Brahmins told the King that this dream was a good omen, and that the child would be holy

What do you think an image like this, which portrays his birth, is trying to say about the importance of Siddhartha?

and achieve perfect wisdom.

Queen Maya entered the garden at Lumbini accompanied by her dancing women and her guards, and walked beneath a sala tree. The tree bent down and the queen took hold of it and looked up to the heavens. At that point Buddha was born out of her side as she stood beneath the tree. He immediately took seven steps towards each quarter of heaven, and at each of these steps there sprung up a lotus flower. He then declared that he would have to experience no more births, that this was his last body and that he would pluck out by the roots the sorrow caused by birth and death.

Queen Maya died seven days after his birth, and Siddhartha was brought up by his aunt (Mahapajapati Gotami), who was also married to his father.

Siddhartha's family belonged to the Kshatriya caste - the second of the castes, often associated with rulers and military leaders. As a Kshatriya, he was allowed to read the scriptures, but not to teach from them. Religious teaching was reserved for Brahmins. One of the major differences between those who were to follow the Buddha and the formal religion of his day was that his followers were treated equally, whatever caste they came from. What mattered was their personal understanding of his teaching and their own spiritual development, not their birth into a particular caste.

As a Kshatriya, Siddhartha would have been expected to follow his father, and take his place as head of the family, and as a local ruler; there is a tradition that, at his birth, a seer called Asita predicted that he would become either a great ruler or a religious teacher. His father, anxious that he should rule, tried to keep all ideas of suffering from his son, for fear that he should start asking too many questions about the meaning of life and become interested in religion.

There are many stories about his youth. They were probably told (and elaborated) in order to contrast his early life with what was to follow. They describe him as a very gifted young man, equally good at sports and the arts. He enjoyed a luxurious lifestyle, including a staff of young women to keep him amused. At the age of sixteen, he was married to a local 'princess' called Yasodhara, and they had a son, Rahula.

Siddhartha as a young ruler. This life of comfort failed to satisfy him.

Siddhartha was also thoughtful and had the ability to become concentrated and absorbed quite happily. Later in life, pondering over his first attempts at disciplined mediation, he thought about some of his childhood experiences and remembered times when he had found himself meditating in a natural and effortless way.

His Religious Quest

Siddhartha is said to have grown dissatisfied. At the age of 29 he started to think seriously about his life and what it meant. In spite of the efforts of his father to protect him from them, he saw four things, while riding out with his charioteer Channa, which changed his life:

1 **An old man** (everyone grows old)
2 **A sick person** (everyone may face disease)
3 **A corpse** (everyone has to die)

At this point, he is described as losing his taste for life. He was unable to enjoy all the luxuries with which he was provided, since he knew that they could not protect him from old age, sickness or death.

4 **A holy man** (one who has devoted himself to the spiritual life: a Sadhu)

This last of the 'four sights' led him to decide that he too would leave home to become a Sadhu, in order to seek a cure for the world's suffering. Once he had seen the facts of life and the scope of human suffering, he felt compelled to do something about it.

In the Hindu tradition, a Sadhu may let his hair grow long as a mark of dedication to the spiritual life.

Siddhartha therefore left his home, rid himself of his fine clothes and set out to become a sadhu. This was not a very unusual thing to do.

There were many wandering religious teachers in India. Some lived on their own, but most gathered around them groups of followers. To start with, Siddhartha went to two different Brahmins, and trained in meditation, but he became dissatisfied with their teachings. He therefore went into the forest and joined a group of ascetics. These were Sadhus who tried to achieve spiritual benefit from living very simply and from treating the body with the strictest discipline.

For six years, Siddhartha followed this way of life. He assumed that the only way to gain spiritual insight was to treat the body severely, until physical needs were reduced to an absolute minimum. It is said that he worked so hard to control is body and its needs, that he nearly starved himself to death. There are images that show him so thin he is almost a skeleton.

He went to bathe in the river Nairanjana and, coming out of the water, he saw Nandabala, the daughter of the overseer of the local cowherds, who offered him a bowl of milk-rice. Siddhartha realised that his ascetic practices could never lead him to full insight. He was too weak even to meditate. So he broke his fast and accepted the milk-rice. His followers thought that this meant he was about to give up all his ascetic disciplines and return to the life of luxury. Disappointed at his apparent failure, they deserted him.

Alone, after six years of his quest, he had still not found an answer to the problem of suffering.

Fact Box

Buddhists believe that, in order to follow the Buddhist path or to meditate, it is necessary to remain healthy and alert, and therefore to take care of your body. You do not get spiritual benefit from depriving your body of what it needs. Self-denial is not of value in itself. Discipline is useful in order to control and direct a person's energies.

The other ascetics continued to think of the body as something impure, to be conquered before a person could make progress. By accepting food, Siddhartha recognised that the body needed to be taken care of.

Activities

Key Elements

1 Where was Siddhartha born?
2 Who were Siddhartha's parents?
3 Who brought Siddhartha up?
4 What does Shakyamuni mean?

5 List his names and titles.
6 What four things made Siddhartha start to think about suffering?
7 What is an ascetic?

Think About It

9 Do you think the story of the birth of Siddhartha is historical fact? If not, what do you think the story is trying to say about the person who was to become the Buddha? List the features of the story that have religious significance.

10 Names used to be very important. Find out about the meaning of your name. Does the meaning suit you? Find out the meanings of more names and rename your friends so that the meanings suit their personalities or physical features.

11 Choosing a name says a lot. Think of suitable names for a) a new chocolate bar, b) a heavy metal band, c) a vegetarian restaurant, d) a new political party. Why did you choose these names?

12 Describe some of the moments in your life which were turning points, when you learnt a lesson about life which has helped you ever since.

13 Siddhartha's life was a bit like a journey. Write a story about a voyage of discovery, including mistakes made on the way.

14 Write an account of any experience you may have had of something that you were determined to do, saying how you felt at every stage. If you cannot think of a personal example, write about what you think it would be like to run a marathon, and why you think so many people want to do that.

Enlightenment

Siddhartha Gautama was 35 years old. He had experienced both wealth and poverty, but neither had given him real satisfaction. He sat in meditation beneath a pipal tree, and determined that he would not move from that place until he had achieved enlightenment.

Fact Box

The word for enlightenment is Bodhi, so the pipal tree under which Gautama sat is called the 'Bodhi tree' (or Bo Tree). Many Buddhist temples have a 'Bo Tree' growing in their grounds, as a reminder of this.

This tree is a reminder to Buddhists of the one under which Siddhartha sat when he became enlightened.

First of all, as he sat in meditation, seeking enlightenment, he had to fight off temptations. A 'devil' figure called Mara is said to have sent images of angry beasts to frighten Gautama, trying to dissuade him from his quest for enlightenment. There were also the sexual temptations of Mara's daughters, trying to make him abandon the quest for the sake of physical and sexual comforts.

When these did not deflect Gautama from his purpose, it is said that Mara tried to sow seeds of doubt in Gautama's mind - doubt about his ability to gain enlightenment.

Mara is said to have demanded a witness to prove that what Gautama had done in his former lives had qualified him to become enlightened.

In response, Gautama is said to have touched the earth, and at that moment the Earth goddess (Vasundhara) appeared and acted as his witness.

Vasundhara represents the supporting and sustaining quality of life and is said to have offered Gautama a vase of amrit (sweetened water) - to invigorate and sustain him (see the illustration). This is said to have happened late in the night, and that from then on Mara retreated in defeat.

It is difficult to convey the content of what Buddha understood as he became enlightened. That is not too surprising, because if a person understood it perfectly, he or she would become enlightened too!

The night was divided up into four periods, in each of which he learned something new:

1 (6 - 10pm) He is said to have gone through various stages of meditation and to have gained knowledge of his former lives (Indian thought includes the idea of rebirth, but most people cannot remember anything of their past lives). In other words, he gained understanding of all the past, and of what had led him to this point of seeking enlightenment.

2 (10pm - 2am) He understood the way in which all creatures come into existence and pass away again. He knew that everything in the world is constantly changing. Nothing lasts forever; however beautiful or precious a thing is, it will eventually change and disappear.

One can enjoy it, but not preserve it for ever.

3 (2-6am) He understood the things that keep creatures bound to the wheel of life - all the negative feelings and cravings that make people grasp at life, even though this brings more suffering. He also knew that he had overcome those cravings.

4 At 6am With the dawn he is said to have gained full enlightenment and experienced the peace of Nirvana (Sk) or Nibbana (P). This is the point at which the three 'fires' (or poisons) of greed, hatred and ignorance are burned out, leaving a sense of happiness and calm.

Activity

Remember a time when you suddenly understood something that previously seemed mysterious to you, or when you suddenly gained insight into another person, changing your view of him or her. Write down what it is like to have such a moment of limited 'enlightenment'.

What is it like to be enlightened?

As we have seen, there is a problem with describing enlightenment - to understand an enlightened mind, you would need to be enlightened yourself! But in the early scriptures (*Majjhima Nikaya*, 39) the Buddha gives descriptions of what it is like to be freed from the hindrances that prevent a person from moving towards enlightenment. Three of them are outlined below. They cannot show what is experienced, but they suggest the sort of feelings that arise when a person enters into deep meditation and therefore give a glimpse of what it would be like to become enlightened.

Suppose you are a slave, perhaps required to carry heavy burdens. Life is painful and you feel trapped in your slavery, unable to go where you want, dependent on others to tell you what to do. Then suddenly you are freed from your slavery: you can put down your burden; you can go where you want; you are independent. You would be overjoyed at that sudden experience of freedom!

Suppose you have been shut up in prison, but suddenly the doors are flung open and you are released. You can reclaim your property, you feel safe and secure, and you can start your life again.

Suppose you have to borrow heavily in order to set yourself up in business. You work hard to make the business succeed, always worried about the debt. Then suddenly the money flows in, you can repay all you owe and still have enough left over to live on. You are no longer in debt, your worries have gone and you are overjoyed.

Question

Look at the hints, given above, about what enlightenment would be like. Have there been any moments in your life when you have felt like that? Describe what it felt like in your own words.

Enlightenenment is not about 'understanding' in the narrow sense of understanding facts. It is a whole new way of seeing and relating to life.

Teaching

For a while after his enlightenment, the Buddha (as Siddhartha can now be called) stayed in the area of Bodh Gaya, meditating. He had to decide whether to keep the new knowledge to himself, or go out and preach. At first he thought other people would not be able to understand it.

One story says that he was approached by Brahma Sahampati (king of the Hindu gods) who begged him to go out and preach. He suggested to the Buddha that the people were like lotus flowers in a lake. Some were still growing up from the mud through the water, but others had reached the surface and some were already clear of the water, about to open their blossoms. In the same way, there were many kinds of people. Not all were stuck in the mud of ignorance; many were just waiting for his teaching in order to blossom out.

Lotuses - and people - growing and developing.

Question

The lotus is an important symbol for Buddhists. From what is said above, or from your previous knowledge of Buddhism, say why you think this is so and what you think each stage in its growth stands for.

Once the Buddha recognised that some people were ready to benefit from his new understanding of life, he felt a strong desire to communicate to them the means by which they too could overcome suffering and achieve peace.

He would have liked to explain his enlightenment to his old meditation teachers, but they had already died. So he set out to find the ascetics who had left him when he gave up his fast.

Upaka

On his way to the Deer Park at Benares, he met a man called Upaka. Like the Buddha before enlightenment, he was a 'holy man' on a spiritual quest (rather than a householder with a family), and he was therefore a likely candidate for receiving the Buddha's teaching.

The Buddha announced to him that he had found the truth, explained the Dharma (teaching) to him, and therefore gave him the opportunity to be his first convert. But Upaka just shrugged his shoulders and walked off!

Life isn't always easy - even for a Buddha!

Sarnath

The Buddha met the five ascetics in the deer park at Sarnath, near Benares. He taught them the Dharma (Teaching), and one by one they became enlightened themselves.

From then on the Buddha started to travel, teach and organise his followers. Many left their homes to follow a similar life to his own, travelling and teaching. Others stayed with their families and occupations, and helped to provide for the wandering teachers.

This is Sarnath, the place where the Buddha first taught the Dharma. Today is a a place of pilgrimage for Buddhists. The photo above shows a huge stupa, a memorial to the Buddha. But Sarnath is not just about remembering the past, it is also a place for Buddhist devotion and celebration. The photo on the left shows Tibetan monks setting out thousands of small butter-oil lamps used to celebrate a visit to Sarnath by the Dalai Lama, their spiritual leader.

For much of each year, his followers went around the towns and villages of northern India, preaching and living off the gifts of food from the people, just like other groups of wandering religious teachers (shramanas). During the rainy season however, it was difficult to travel, so the full-time Buddhist preachers would meet together for study and meditation. Some wealthy followers gave pieces of land to the Buddha and his full-time preachers so that they could have regular places to gather.

During the Buddha's lifetime there were therefore two kinds of followers:

1. those who joined him in the wandering shramana life, but who gathered together from time to time. Gradually, they started to spend more of their time in their meeting places, and became monks and nuns.

2. householders, who accepted his teaching, continued with their normal lives, and supported the travelling preachers in various ways. They are generally known as lay Buddhists.

Activities

Key Elements

1 Why could Siddhartha not be called the Buddha before his enlightenment?
2 Where did the Buddha first preach?
3 What is the difference between a monk and a lay Buddhist?
4 What did the monks do during the rainy season?

Think about it

5 Why might a lay Buddhist want to become a monk? Why might another decide to remain a lay follower?

The Buddhist scriptures give many stories about the Buddha meeting people and the effect he had upon them. Most of them say that the Buddha was teaching in such and such a place, and that someone came to him with a problem, or to ask a question about his teaching. He then gave that person a teaching, and he or she responded, sometimes by going back to the same life but with a new insight, sometimes by changing the way he or she was living, and sometimes by giving everything up and following the Buddha in his life of wandering and teaching. Other stories - like the one illustrated below - show his practical concern for people, and the sort of advice he gave his followers

The Death of the Buddha

The Buddha dies, surrounded by his followers. The last thing he said to them was a reminder that all things are subject to change (a central feature of his teaching - see chapter two) and that his followers should strive on with mindfulness (an idea we shall examine in chapter four). This painting is in a temple in Kandy, Sri Lanka.

The Buddha spend about 45 years travelling and teaching. Finally, old and weak, he died of food poisoning at Kushinara. One of the Buddhist scriptures (the *Parinibbana Sutta*) is devoted to the events and teaching of the last period of the Buddha's life.

By the time he died, he had become the leader of a very large religious movement, and had become well known throughout northern India.

The Buddha was cremated, but his bones remained unburned. There was some dispute about who should have them, but eventually they were distributed among various rulers of the tribes and kingdoms, who built monuments (stupas) over them.

Activities

Key Elements

1 For how many years did the Buddha preach?

2 Where did he die?

3 Which scripture is devoted to the Buddha's last teachings?

4 What happened to his remains?

Think About It

4 Look at the image of the dying Buddha at the top of the page. What does this suggest to you about the Buddhist view of death?

5 Write an obituary for the Buddha, for an imaginary local newspaper in Kushinara.

Other Buddhas

'Buddha' is the term used for an enlightened being and although Siddhartha Gautama is seen as the Buddha for this present age, he is not generally thought of as the only one.

Early Buddhist traditions include the idea of Maitreya (Sk) or Metteya (P), a Buddha who will appear in the future in order to restore the teaching (Dharma) once it has died out on Earth. Later Buddhist writings (e.g. the Lotus Sutra, see page 63) see the universe as made up of thousands of millions of worlds, in each of which there is a Buddha teaching.

All Buddhas are believed to teach the same truth, but each adapting it to the needs of a particular time and place.

Buddha images

Buddha images are visual aids. They express qualities of the Buddha and are a means by which Buddhists can remind themselves of those qualities and also express their devotion to the Buddha and his teaching - for example, by offering candles, incense or flowers before an image at a shrine.

There are many different kinds of Buddha image. Some depict Siddhartha, but others represent one of the many other Buddha figures. Each shows something about enlightenment, by illustrating calmness, or fearlessness, or energy or compassion. In chapters 8 and 9 we shall be looking at some of these images and what they stand for.

Activities

Think About It

1   Are there any skills or qualities you would like to develop? Play a musical instrument, for example? Improve your handwriting? Run faster? Become wiser? More compasionate? How could you go about doing this?

Assignments

1   The story of the Buddha's life is like the story of a journey. Read one of the following books and write a review of it: *Pilgrim's Progress*; *Monkey*; *The Wizard of Oz*. What sort of journey does it describe? (In *The Wizard of Oz*, the Scarecrow is looking for a brain, the Tin Man for a heart and the Lion for courage. They hope the Wizard will help them but on the journey they find that they already have these qualities and didn't know it. Three qualities of Buddhahood are said to be Wisdom, Compassion and Courage. Dorothy is looking for her home, and is told at the end that she has had the power to get there all along. What does this tell you about Buddhism?)

2   Design symbols to represent the stages to enlightenment. Put them together to make a poster.

3   What, if anything, do you see as the appeal of the ascetic tradition which Gautama followed for seven years before his enlightenment?

4   Immediately before his enlightenment, Gautama is described as being attacked by the temptations of Mara. How might such temptations be described today?

The Dharma

- The Three Marks of Existence
- The Four Noble Truths
- The Noble Eightfold Path
- The Self

- Karma
- Samsara and Rebirth
- What Counts as Dharma?
- The Wheel of Life

Fact Box
'Dharma' (Sk) or 'Dhamma' (P) is a word with many meanings. It is sometimes used as 'reality' or even 'thing' - so it is possible to speak of 'understanding all dharmas', or to think of Dharma as the truth about the way the world works (something like 'The Law of Life'). But for Buddhism it also means 'teaching'. When a Buddhist speaks 'practising the Dharma', it is the teaching of the Buddha and his followers that he or she means. In fact, 'Buddhism' is a Western term for the religion of those who follow the Buddha's teaching, Buddhists themselves generally speak of what they do as simply 'practising the Dharma'.

Every image expersses some particular feature of Enlightenment or the Buddha's life. The hand position here shows that this is an image of him teaching (see page 111).

For more than forty years after his enlightenment, the Buddha travelled round Northern India. He taught a wide variety of people, often giving a teaching in response to a question that someone asked him. He did not simply offer a set of ideas, but a way of thinking and acting that aimed to help individuals to gain enlightenment.

The Buddha described his teaching as being like a raft that a person used to cross a river. A raft is not something which you simply sit and look at, nor is it sensible to carry the raft with you once you have crossed the river. It is something to be used and then set aside.

His followers memorised and repeated his teaching, although it was to be about 400 years before it was written down.

In this chapter we shall be looking at the main features of the Dharma.

The Three Marks of Existence.

Buddha taught that everything comes into existence, because of certain conditions. Once those conditions change, then it ceases to exist. For example, we can live only while there is oxygen in the air for us to breathe; without it, we would cease to exist. Everything is therefore dependent upon other things - nothing exists on its own account.

Alone, in a desert, without water, you would quickly understand that you depend on many things outside yourself.

The Buddha applied this idea to all aspects of life - both physical and spiritual (personal and religious). Neither his life of luxury nor his life as an ascetic had given him the right conditions under which he could gain insight or experience genuine happiness.

The Dharma therefore seeks to create the conditions - through mental training, morality and insight - which enable people to grow and to experience freedom and happiness.

But in order to understand how Buddhism proposes to do this, it is important to look at the basic conditions under which people live. The Buddha taught three '**marks of conditioned existence**' (sometimes called the three '**universal truths**'):

1. *Anicca:* All things are constantly changing - nothing is fixed. Everything depends on conditions, which themselves can change.

Nothing is permanent: even stars and galaxies are gradually changing. Galaxies are formed by conditions which will eventually change.

2. *Anatta:* There is a tradition that anatta was the subject of the Buddha's second sermon to the five ascetics, after which they all achieved enlightenment. Anatta means 'no permanent identity', or 'no separate self'. All beings are interdependent, none can exist separately from the others, and therefore none of them is fixed and unchanging. When applied to human beings it means that, as conditions change, so people too will change. Anatta can be taken more generally to mean that nothing whatever, in the ordinary world of our experience, has a fixed or permanent nature.

Activity
As a group, collect photographs of each person as a baby and mix them up. Try to work out which photo belongs to which person. What things about them are the same? What has changed?

---

3. *Dukkha:* If life is always changing, all that we know and love will eventually cease to exist. We ourselves are liable to suffer from disease, and even if we escape illnesses and accidents, we will one day have to face the certainty of old age and death.

Dukkha means 'suffering'. It refers to this general fact of disease, old age and death, but also to the sense that the world is unsatisfactory - that in itself it cannot give people the permanent happiness that they seek.

Buddhism aims to help you straighten out your wheel.

Fact Box

It is possible that the word *dukkha* came from *du-* (bad, or ill-fitting) and the second part of the word *cakka* (wheel) -referring to a badly fitted chariot wheel. A dukkha will slow down your progress, and make your journey through life rather uncomfortable!

Thinking about these three marks of existence, a Buddhist might say: -

Since everything around you changes, and since you also change, it is foolish to rely on or cling to things around you, expecting them to give you permanent happiness. This only leads to suffering. Learn how to enjoy things just as they are, without trying to own them or stop them from changing.

Activities

Key Elements

1 What do Buddhists usually call their religion?
2 What meanings does the word 'dharma' have?

3 Put the following into your own words, and give an example of each of them to illustrate its meaning: Anicca; Anatta; Dukkha.

Think About It

4 Think of things or people you depended on when you were younger. Do you still depend on them in the same way? What would your life be like if you did?
5 Make a list of all the things in the world that you depend on for your life. Which of them depend on something else? (e.g you depend on food, food depends on plants, plants depend on sunlight...) Which of them could change? How could that change come about?

6 Buddhists claim that their religion offers people the opportunity to discover freedom and happiness. Do you think this is possible if the world in which we live is unsatisfactory and if all life involves suffering?
7 List the things that make you unhappy. Is there anything you can do to stop them making you unhappy? What things make you happy? How can you hold on to that happiness?

The Four Noble Truths

By tradition, the Four Noble Truths were the subject of the first sermon (or teaching) given by the Buddha to the five ascetics in the Deer Park at Sarnath - an event which is generally known as 'Setting in Motion the Wheel of the Dharma'.

In it the Buddha set out:
- the problem with life
- the cause of that problem
- that the problem can be overcome
- the way to achieve it.

The problem he tackles is suffering, and the aim is to overcome it, promoting insight, peace and happiness. His argument follows the idea that everything depends on conditions, and it is set out in the way that traditional Indian medicine set out the nature of a disease and the way to be cured of it. The Buddha argued that if you want to remove suffering, you must examine the conditions that lead to it.

He set out the way to do this in four stages: - 'The Four Noble Truths':

1. All life involves suffering.

Suffering is *dukkha* - the third of the 'marks of conditioned existence'. This refers to several different things. First there is the actual pain and distress that comes because of sickness, old age, death and all the other injuriries that can come to human beings. Dukkha of this sort is inevitable because we are limited and fragile beings.

Some forms of suffering can't be avoided; they are part of being human. Buddhism does not claim to prevent you from breaking a leg or from dying.

Then there is the sense of frustration and unhappiness with life - that nothing is ever exactly as we might wish it to be. The Dharma also says that there are three 'poisons' which lead to more and more suffering - they are **ignorance**, **greed** and **hatred**.

2. The origin of suffering is craving.

The word used for craving is *tanha*. This is not the natural need for food and the other necessities of life, nor is it the enjoyment that comes from pleasant experiences. It is the attempt to grasp at the things we enjoy, to try to own them, to stop them from changing, to want more and more of them. This grasping shows that people feel a kind of inner emptiness and want to fill it. The more they grasp, the more they suffer.

Activities

- Which forms of suffering cannot be changed? Which can be changed, at least to some extent? Make two lists.

- Think of examples of people craving for things and being disappointed or suffering as a result. Then write down:
  1. Why you think they craved for them in the first place.
  2. What effect the craving had.
  3. What this tells you about human life.

3. The end of suffering (niroda).

The Buddha taught that the only way to end suffering was to stop craving and grasping at life (*niroda* means 'cessation'). But a person who feels emotionally empty will want to grasp. Therefore the only way to stop craving is to discover inner satisfaction, and an appreciation of life as it really is, so that there is no need to grasp. If Buddhists are able to reduce their craving (*tanha*), it is because they enjoy life and do not need to crave for more - so ceasing to crave is a positive step and not a negative one.

The point at which all craving ceases is a point of peace called Nibbana (P) or Nirvana (Sk). The Buddha is said to have achieved this state at his enlightenment - and that many of his followers also became similarly freed from craving. A person who has achieved nirvana may still carry on living, eating, having relationships with other people (as the Buddha did for forty five years after his enlightenment) but his or her actions would be done from a selfless motive, not from craving, and therefore they do not lead to further suffering.

Nirvana is not the same thing as extinction. Indeed, the Buddha saw 'craving for extinction' as selfish. Nirvana does not mean being so removed from life that you feel nothing! Rather, it describes a state of peace and happiness.

Those who have achieved nirvana still experience things that others see as pain and pleasure, but they do not respond to them as they would if they were unenlightened. For an enlightened person, pleasure or pain will not be the cause of yet more craving and suffering.

4. The Way that leads to the cessation of suffering

This is 'The Middle Way' (*Magga*), and it is often set out in the form of a path of eight steps. These are not meant to be steps that a person has to take one after another, but eight features of the Buddhist life.

Fact Box

Buddhism is like a path or journey. It is something to be done, not just something to be believed.

A person becomes a Buddhist by following the Buddha and his teachings in the company of others.

There are many different ways of setting out the Buddhist path, of which one of the best known in 'The Noble Eightfold Path' to be outlined on the next page.

Activities

Key Elements

1. Put the Four Noble Truths in your own words.

Think About It

2. Write down what you think happiness is. List the things that make you happy. Would you still be able to be happy if these things were taken away from you?

3. Why do you think one person may be happy and another unhappy in the same circumstances?

The Noble Eightfold Path

There are three aspects to the Buddhist way of life:
1 Wisdom (*prajna*)
2 Morality (*sila*)
3 Mental training (*samadhi*)
and the Noble Eightfold Path deals with all three.

The way of wisdom -

1 Right (or perfect) view
A Buddhist seeks to deepen his or her understanding of life, following the teachings of the Buddha. A person who has not thought about the nature or conditioned existence or the origin of suffering, is unlikely to make progress. This is not just book-learning, but a personal view of what life is about. Without such a view, there would be little point in trying to follow the path at all.

2 Right (or perfect) intention
It is one thing to hear the Buddhist Dharma, quite another to actually decide to act on it, and to do so for the right reasons. 'Right intention' is a decision to follow the Buddhist path, both for the sake of your own freedom and eventual enlightenment, but also out of an unselfish love for all beings. Every action a person does springs from some thought, and this right intention is the positive thought that a person needs in order to make progress.

> Remember Upaka, the first *sadhu* to whom the Buddha explained the Dharma, while on his way to Sarnath. He simply shrugged his shoulders and went on his way. He lacked 'right intention'!

Remember:
Although the way of wisdom comes first, you do not have to become wise before starting on the rest of the path. For most people, the way of morality is the starting point.

The way of morality -

3 Right (or perfect) speech
Buddhists should avoid four kinds of speech:
1 telling lies
2 causing trouble between people by spreading gossip
3 speaking harshly
4 time-wasting chatter.
because these may cause suffering to oneself and to others. Rather, they should always try:
- to be truthful, careful and accurate in what they say
- to speak in a way that promotes harmony between people
- to be kind and gentle in their speech
- to value silence, when there is nothing useful to say.

4 Right (or perfect) Action
All Buddhists try to follow five 'precepts' - general guidelines for life. They are:
1 not to destroy life
2 not to steal
3 not to misuse sex, or over-indulge the senses
4 not to lie (already part of 'right speech')
5 not to cloud the mind with drugs or alcohol
(We shall examine these in more detail in chapter six. There are other precepts and rules, in addition to these, for those who are ordained or who become monks and nuns.)

5 Right (or perfect) livelihood
If a person follows the Buddhist path, it is important that he or she should earn a living in a way that does not involve going against Buddhist principles. Work should be of benefit, and should not harm others. (We shall examine this idea in chapter six.)

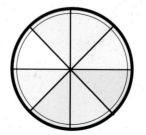

The Dharma is sometimes represented as a wheel with eight spokes - one for each of the steps of the Noble Eightfold Path.

The way of mental training -

6 Right (or perfect) effort

The first, and most obvious step to take in training the mind is to make a conscious effort to set aside all negative, evil thoughts, and to replace them by good and positive ones. It is not expected that a Buddhist will achieve this all at once! But this step recognises that a Buddhist should be aware of and make an effort to shape the way in which he or she habitually thinks. By following this step, a Buddhist will always try to see good in others.

7 Right (or perfect) mindfulness

Part of the mental training in the Buddhist way of life aims to help people become more aware of themselves and of everything around them. People cannot control or develop themselves if they are unaware of how they actually feel, or why they respond to life as they do. Equally, people are unlikely to help others if they are lost in the world of their own rather than seeing what is happening around them. Buddhists practise meditation to help them to be aware in this way.

8 Right (or perfect) concentration

We shall look at mediation techniques and other forms of spiritual practice in chapter four. Buddhists believe that through meditation the mind is enabled to become calm, to develop loving-kindness, and also to gain insight into the truths of life. The ultimate goal of this process of *nirvana*, but regular meditation is an important part of the life of every practising Buddhist.

Fact Box

The Eightfold Path is not the only way to set out the Buddhist spiritual path. There are other lists too, for example:

The 'seven limbs of enlightenment' -
1) mindfulness 2) correct doctrine 3) effort 4) joy 5) tranquility 6) meditation 7) even-mindedness.

The 'five powers' -
1) faith 2) vigour 3) mindfulness 4) concentration 5) wisdom.

These lists do not conflict with one another - they are simply convenient, but different ways of bringing together the various aspects of what the Buddhist journey towards enlightenment can involve

---

Activities

Key Elements

1 Write out the stages of the Noble Eightfold Path. Against each stage, write down an example of how it could be applied to your own life.

Think about it

2 In what ways would your life change if you followed the Noble Eightfold Path? Which steps would you find most difficult?

The Self

One of the marks of conditioned existence was *anatta* (no fixed self). So what is a human being?

In *The Questions of King Milinda*, a Buddhist teacher, Nagasena wants to show the King that the self is made up of different things, and that there is no 'soul' that is the 'real' self. He uses the image of the chariot being made up of wheels, an axle etc., no one thing being the 'real' chariot. In the same way, a person an be analysed into skin, bone, blood etc., without ever finding the 'real' self.

Buddhists describe human beings as being made up of five 'heaps' called the five skandhas.

The five Skandhas

A human being may be described as comprising five *skandhas* (literally: heaps).
They are:

Form: our physical element

Sensations: the feelings we have as our senses contact the outside world.

Perceptions: what we become aware of as our senses give us information.

Mental Formations / impulses: what we decide to do and think as a result of all this.

Consciousness: the basic awareness of being alive, with thoughts and feelings.

All of these skandhas are changing all the time - there is no permanent and unchanging self. A person consists of these five 'heaps' - they come together in a unique combination when a person is born, and they fall apart again when that person dies.

> ### Activity
> Write down a description of a friend without saying what he or she looks like. What sort of things have you described?

Karma

How do we influence the process of change? Is there anything that we can do to shape the future? The answer to this question is given in the idea of '*karma*', or 'The Law of Karma'. This can best be summed up as 'actions have consequences'. A person's karma is the accumulated effect of his or her actions.

Karma is not generated by every action, but only by those that are 'ethically significant' - in other words, those what reflect personal attitudes and choices.

In the Dhammapada (an early collection of the Buddha's teachings) it is put like this:

> *What we are today comes from our thoughts of yesterday, and our present thoughts build our life of tomorrow: our life is the creation of our mind. ...If a man speaks or acts with an impure mind, suffering follows him as the wheel of the cart follows the beast that draws the cart. ...if a man speaks and acts with a pure mind, joy follows him as his own shadow.*
> *(Dhammapada 1,2)*

> ### Fact Box
> Buddhists do not believe in a god who rewards or punishes people for what they do. A person's *karma* is not a punishment or reward given by some outside force, but simply the natural result of everything that he or she has done.

There are different ways of describing how Karma works. Here are two comments by a Buddhist monk:

The memory of what you have done wrong is the karmic effect of it

Kamma is what you do now, because of what you did then.

Therefore, a person who bears grudges, or who has unhappy memories that stir up feelings of hatred or resentment, is likely to act in a way that reflects that negative karma (Sk), or kamma (P). On the other hand, a person who is able to forgive what has happened in the past - accepting and understanding it - becomes free from its negative effects.

There is also good, or positive, karma - a kindly action will eventually bear fruit, even if its result is not immediately obvious.

Activities

Here are two examples of actions and their consequenes:

- Many people who abuse their children have themselves been the victims of abuse in their childhood.
- Those who are addicted to drugs sometimes steal in order to pay for yet more drugs, and so on.

• Write down other examples to illustrate *karma* - and its effects, both good and bad.

But not every hateful action leads to another. Sometimes people are able to make a new start - to overcome negative karma from their past. This is breaking out of the cycle of actions and their consequences through which the world continually adds to its sufferings.

• Imagine and write down a situation in which someone breaks out of the cycle of suffering and makes a new start. Try and say how he or she might feel, and how difficult it would be to break the cycle.

Activities

Key Elements

1 What is the literal meaning of *karma*?

2 What does *karma* mean for a Buddhist?

Think About it

3 How might a Buddhist explain why some people choose to do wrong, and yet seem to get away with it?

4 Do you think that the idea of karma explains everything that happens to

people? What other explanations can you think of?

5 Is there such a thing as coincidence? What would a Buddhist say?

Samsara and Rebirth

In order to be able to communicate his teaching, the Buddha had to use words and ideas that his hearers would understand. Buddhism therefore takes over many features of Hindu thought. At the time of the Buddha, one of the ideas that was gaining popularity was that the world was like a great wheel of life and death - with creatures constantly being born, growing old, dying, and being born again. This was known as the world of *samsara* - and it was a world of suffering and death from which it was hoped that a person might eventually escape. The Hindu belief was that everyone had a soul (*atman*) which moved on to inhabit another body after death.

The Buddha accepted some of these ideas, but modified them. For Buddhists, rebirth - or 're-becoming' - is a constant process of change. What a person will be later, develops out of what he or she has been before. This is believed to happen throughout life, but can it go beyond this life?

We have already seen that the Buddha taught *anatta* - no fixed self - so how can there be re-birth? What is there to move from one life to another?

If we are constantly being re-formed as the result of our *karma*, then, when we come to the end of our present life, there is likely to be a great deal of *karma* - through actions we have done, words we have spoken - which has not yet produced its results. A Buddhist might say that this karma goes on to be worked out in future lives, which are therefore linked to our own in that way.

Some Buddhists go further and say that the last act of consciousness of one life leads on to the first one of the next and that people can sometimes remember past lives. We shall see in the chapter of Tibetan Buddhism that when a senior teacher dies a hunt is made for the child who is born to take on his karma.

In the book *The Questions of King Milinda*, the Buddhist sage Nagasena (2nd century BCE) uses images to describe how one life leads into another.

- imagine the flame of one lamp lighting another. It is not the same flame in the second lamp, but it has come about because of the first.

- milk, curds, butter and ghee are all the same thing, but one changes into the next depending on different conditions.

In the same way, although there is no soul to pass from one life to another, Buddhists see the future as arising out of the present.

Fact Box

The world of suffering and change (*Samsara*) is contrasted with *Nirvana* - the state of peace brought about by the absence of hatred, greed and ignorance. But this does not mean that there are two different **places** - they are two different ways of seeing and experiencing life.

Activities

Key Elements

1 What is samsara? Describe it in your own words.

Think About It

2 Why do you think Buddhist funerals are joyful occasions?

3 How might the Buddhist teachings help a person to face death?

What Counts as Dharma?

In this chapter we have looked at some of the things that the Buddha taught. But it is also important to be aware of what he did **not** teach. He refused to answer the following questions:

1 Is the universe eternal, or did it start and will it end?
2 Is the universe infinite, or does it have limits?
3 Is the life of a human being to be identified with the physical person?
4 Does an enlightened being exist or not exist after death?

Now these are the questions that people in the West tend to assume religion is about. Why did the Buddha not spend his time trying to answer them?

• He said that he could give no straightforward answers to these questions, because they are asked by people whose minds are limited. If they were told the answers to them, they would not be able to understand them. (This does not mean that they are not interesting to think about, but that you may need to change your views as you develop greater insight. There is no simple answer that is right for everyone.)

• He said that these questions were irrelevant to the main purpose of his life and teaching - which was to help people overcome suffering and achieve happiness. (In other words, the Buddhist path is a practical way of deepening an understanding of life as we experience it here and now. To worry about questions to which we cannot know the answers is a distraction and a waste of time.)

So the Buddha did not claim to teach about everything - but only about those things that a person needed to know in order to make progress in overcoming suffering and achieving happiness.

A popular Buddhist image for this is of the man who has been shot with an arrow. There is no point in sitting round discussing what kind of arrow it is, or who shot it - the first thing to do is actually to get the arrow out of his body.

In the same way, Buddhist teaching does not aim to provide interesting topics for discussion, but simply a way of understanding life that may lead to peace, happiness and insight into the way things really are.

Fact Box

Because Buddha did not give answers to all these things, people were free to follow his teaching but at the same time continue with some of the religious practices of the culture in which they lived. This is still true today. In China, for example, people who became Buddhist continued to have ideas from Confucianism and Taoism. In some southern Buddhist countries, there are shrines for the worship of local gods and spirits. This is not part of Buddhism, but those who wish to continue with these traditions do so. They do no harm, according to Buddhism, as long as they do not conflict with Buddhist teaching, and as long as people do not put their trust in them, or expect them to work through some kind of magic.

Although there seems to be a great deal of Dharma, as far as a Buddhist is concerned, the test for what he or she needs to know at any stage in the path is simple. When asked by his aunt and foster-mother Mahapajapati how she could tell what was the true Dharma, the Buddha said:

> "Whatever leads to purity.... to freedom ... to decrease in worldly gains and acquisitions ... to simplicity ... to contentment ... to individuality ... to energy ... to delight in the good... that is the Dharma"

Buddhist *dharma* is like a raft that a person uses in order to cross a river. Its purpose is a practical one - it is there in order to help a person to achieve happiness and insight. There are no prizes in Buddhism for believing impossible things. Buddhists are expected to examine and test out the Buddha's teachings to find out for themselves whether they are true to their own experience.

The Wheel of Life

The Wheel of Life illustrates life in the world of *samsara*. It is found especially in Tibetan Buddhism, but the ideas it sets out are common to all Buddhist traditions.

Buddhists will look carefully at the Wheel of Life, using it like a mirror in which they see reflected aspects of their own lives. Each image within the Wheel represents one particular feature of life and the wheel as a whole shows how they are connected to one another.

In the hub of the wheel are three creatures - a cock, a snake and a pig - which represent greed, hatred and ignorance. (Often called the 'Three Mental Poisons'.) Each bites the other's tail, suggesting that these three things feed on one another. The world of *samsara* is kept turning by these three things, and Buddhists see them as the starting point of all human problems.

Outside this hub is a circle which is divided into two. On one side men and women, in various states of unhappiness and torment are falling downwards. On the other, happy figures are moving upwards. This represents the changes that can happen as conditions (and responses to them) change.

Next there is a circle divided into six segments. These represent six realms. They are:

1 **the realm of the gods** - this is a beautiful dream-world where everything is provided.

   [Some Buddhists do speak of gods - but only as beings who are superior to humans, but not enlightened. They are not as important as the Buddha and they are **not** the same as 'God' in Western religions.]

2 **the realm of** *asuras* - angry beings that are constantly at war with one another, fighting to get what they want.

3 **the realm of** *pretas* **(hungry ghosts) -** beings who always want more and are never satisfied. They have enormous stomachs, with knives sticking out of them, and tiny mouths.

4 **the hell realms -** some are hot, some cold; all express human suffering and despair.

5 **the animal realm -** where the main concern is the basic requirements of food and sex and material comfort. Beings in this realm seem to be quite happy as long as their needs are being met.

6 **the human realm.**

By tradition, beings do not remain permanently in any one of those realms, but move from one to another. Buddhists do not see these as separate places, but as different conditions in which people live, or different states of mind.

Then there is the outermost circle which comprises twelve scenes, depicting what Buddhists call the twelve *nidanas* (links). These are said to illustrate the way in which one thing arises because of another - and therefore why the whole wheel of samsara keeps moving round.

1 a blind man - He represents spiritual ignorance.

2 a potter at work - Because of ignorance, people make choices and start to create *karma*.

3 a monkey climbing a tree - This represents the start of consciousness of a new life.

4 a boat with four passengers - This is the new body, along with its feelings, perceptions and acts of will.

5 an empty house with five windows and a door - this represents the five senses, plus the mind, with which everyone is equipped.

6 a couple embracing one another - a person's senses make contact with their objects, and form a relationship with them.

7 a man with an arrow in his eye - contact with objects leads to feelings - pleasant, painful or neutral.

8 a woman offering a drink to a man - feelings lead to thirst, or craving.

9 a man gathering fruit - because of their feelings, people become attached to things and ideas and crave them.

10 a pregnant woman - attachment leads to more life, the Buddhist term for this is *bhava*, which means 'becoming'.

11 childbirth - 'becoming' leads on to the arising of a new life

12 a corpse - everything that is born, eventually has to die, and the wheel of conditioned existence has completed its cycle.

In a visual way, these links show that, as one life emerges, it develops senses that reach out and start to grasp at things outside itself. This grasping leads to the desire for more life, and the cycle starts all over again.

Around the outside of the Wheel of Life is a monster representing death. And then, outside the wheel, is an image of the Buddha.

The Wheel of Life includes the idea that there is a chance for people to escape from the endless round of life, death and craving. The point of escape is between the seventh and eighth links on the outermost wheel -- the point between having pleasant or painful experiences, and reacting to those experiences by craving and grasping at life.

If a person stops craving, then the outermost circle stops revolving, and he or she can escape from its consequences. It also means that, of all the realms, it is the human one that offers that chance of escape, for it is only by making a mature human decision not to react to life by craving and grasping, that a person can escape.

Fact Box

The Wheel of Life is an image of what life is like and a means of reflecting on various aspects of experience. It is a way of showing how people respond to situations. It does NOT claim to represent a literal view of the external world, but is more like a 'mind map' to guide you through your hopes and fears, your choices and their consequences.

Activity

Write a story to illustrate how a person may travel through each of these realms.

Activities

Key Elements

1   What are the Three Mental Poisons?
2   What is the connection between these three things and suffering?

3   What are the nidanas? Explain them in your own words.

Think About It

4   Give examples of the sort of people you would expect to find in each of the six realms. Which of the realms do you think you are in most of the time?

5   In each of the six realms there is said to be a Buddha at work. Why do you think this is? What would he be trying to do?

Assignments

1   Some people say that Buddhism is not a religion, but a philosophy of life. What do you think? (First of all, you will need to decide what a religion is.)
2   Write down a list of different forms of suffering that human beings can experience. Against each one write down what you think causes it. Then say what you think a Buddhist would have to say about it.
3   Design a poster which shows the connection between the Three Marks of Existence, the Four Noble Truths and the Noble Eightfold Path.

The Sangha

Fact Box

Sangha means Assembly - a group of people - and it is used to describe the community of people who follow the Buddha and his teachings (Dharma). Sometimes *Sangha* refers to the Order of Buddhist monks, but more generally it can mean all those who practise Buddhism.

The Dharma could not have been taught without the Buddha, and could not be followed without the Sangha. Therefore, the Buddha, the Dharma and the Sangha are inseparable: each depends on the other two.

Together, the Buddha, the Dharma and Sangha are called the Tiratana (P) or Triratna (Sk). These three things are so special to Buddhists that they are often known as the Three Jewels or the Three Treasures.

The Three Refuges

In India at the time of Siddhartha there were many travelling religious teachers, and they all had followers of various kinds. Some followers enjoyed the novelty, some liked a good argument, and Siddhartha no doubt had his share of these. But many of the Buddha's followers were people who were genuinely seeking to learn the truth about life. These people became committed to the Buddha's teaching and asked to be accepted as disciples. However, they did not just join together as a group, they personally devoted themselves to the Buddha and his teachings. In other words, they took refuge in the Buddha, the Dharma and the Sangha.

The Sangha was organised during the Buddha's own lifetime. Converts who wanted to join the Buddha in a full time religious quest became known as Bhikkus (P). Bhikku is often translated as monk or priest, but it really means far more than this. The Buddha said:-"A man who wishes to be my disciple must be willing to give up all direct relations with his family, the social life of the world and all dependence on wealth." Bhikkus should try to live exactly as the Buddha did. The function of the Sangha was made clear when the Buddha first sent his Bhikkus into the world. He said:- "Go out on your journey for the profit of many, out of compassion for the world for the welfare and bliss of mankind. Proclaim the Dharma."

Question

- What do the following words mean?
Compassion
Welfare
Bliss

    Write down their meanings and say how each of them relates to the teaching of the Buddha.

These first missionaries were given the authority to admit new believers to the Sangha if it was requested. This was done by reciting a formula which is still used by Buddhists today. In Pali it runs:

Buddham saranam gacchami
Dhammam saranam gacchami
Sangham saranam gacchami.

[Before reading on, can you work out what this formula means? The words 'saranam gacchami' mean 'I take refuge in'.]

In English the formula runs:-
I take refuge in the Buddha
I take refuge in the Dharma
I take refuge in the Sangha

This formula is known as Tisarana (P). It is not the purpose of the bhikku to convert anyone. He takes refuge in the Three Jewels and regards the Dharma as the Law of Life itself. He therefore believes that it is his duty to teach the Dharma to others, but then it is up to each individual to practise Buddhism or not.

Spot the difference. Which teacher is the bhikku like?

Question

- Some words go together so that they are defined in terms of each other. e.g Aunt = female who has a nephew; nephew = male who has an aunt. Aunt and nephew are ideas which cannot be separated. The same applies to the The Three Jewels. Define each of them in terms of the other two.

Women in the Sangha

When asked by his cousin Ananda, the Buddha made it clear that women as well as men were able to achieve enlightenment. The Sangha was open to both men and women, and women who joined the monastic Sangha as nuns were called Bhikkunis (P) or Bhikshunis (Sk).

However, this was not an easy step for him to take and the Buddha was at first unwilling to allow women to join as nuns. He expected them to practise the Dharma within their family life. It was only after his Aunt and foster-mother, Mahapajapati, was absolutely determined to keep asking for ordination, that he accepted that women could 'go forth' from home into the homeless life. In this he was being very radical, for in India at that time women were expected to be concerned with home and family, not to live as homeless preachers.

He might have been reluctant to accept women into the homeless life in case they were asking for the wrong reasons. Religious teachers and sadhus were held in very great respect, whereas women generally had a far lower place in society. Some women might have been tempted to see becoming a nun as a way of gaining a social status that they could not achieve in the home.

Some women were very influential within the Sangha. One of his early followers, Dhammadinna, became particularly skilled in explaining the Dharma and was highly respected. One of the sections in the early Buddhist scriptures records her teachings.

Activity

Write or act out a debate between two women, both of whom are early followers of the Buddha. One wants to 'go forth', the other thinks it right to stay at home.

Before a person becomes a full monk or nun, he or she will generally spend two years as an anagarika (see page 74). Anagarikas wear white robes. Nuns wear the same sort of robes as monks, but may decide to have a different colour. Some nuns wear deep brown. Monks and nuns share practical jobs round the monastery on the basis of each person's ability, not their sex. Both monks and nuns receive gifts of food from lay people.

Activities

Key Elements

1 What are the Three Jewels?

2 What is a Buddhist monk called?

3 What is the Tisarana?

4 What does it mean to 'go for refuge'?

Think About It

5 The Buddha said, "He who sees the Dharma sees me; he who sees me sees the Dharma." What do you think he meant by that?

6 If the Buddha had lived in the West today, how do you think he would have responded to the request that women should become nuns?

The Councils

After the Buddha's death, it was feared that people would be tempted to worship him rather than simply following his teachings. Also, in order to preserve his teachings faithfully, it was important to agree on them and compile them. This was done by calling conferences of those who heard the teachings originally, and these conferences were called Councils.

The First Council for the compilation of the Buddha's teachings is believed to have taken place at Rajagaha in Eastern India about three months after the Buddha's death. Five hundred bhikkus attended and the elder disciples recited the teachings as they had heard them. Upali was very disciplined and was able to repeat the rules and regulations that the Buddha had laid down for the Sangha. Ananda had accompanied the Buddha for a long time and so could recite the Buddha's teachings on doctrine. Once the members of the Council agreed on the accuracy of the remembered teachings, they recited them together, but they were not written down for hundreds of years.

Discuss

In India at that time, the spoken word was considered to be far more important than the written word, so important religious teachings were often not written down, but passed on by word of mouth. Can you suggest why this may have been so?

A hundred years later a Second Council of the Sangha met at Vesali. At this sitting, some members voiced the opinion that many of the existing rules of the Sangha were unnecessarily rigid and restrictive. For example, one rule stated that the Bhikkus were prohibited from eating after midday; another forbade them from accepting gifts of money. Progressive members of the Council proposed that the rules be relaxed a little. In fact they argued that the Buddha had suggested this himself just before he died. The Elders of the Sangha disagreed, saying that observing the rules strictly was the certain way to attain Buddhahood.

The conflict was never resolved, and the Sangha split into two groups. The more conservative bhikkus who observed the rules very strictly included those who followed the Theravada or 'Teaching of the Elders' tradition. The progressive and more tolerant bhikkus called themselves the Mahasanghika or 'Members of the Great Sangha'.

After the Second Council, the two groups had further disagreements between themselves. They divided and subdivided until by the end of the first century BCE there were eighteen or twenty different groups within the Buddhist religion. Although they disagreed about the correct way to follow the Buddhist path, they still thought of themselves as belonging to one Sangha, and monks of different traditions lived and worked alongside one another in the same monasteries.

Activities

Key Elements

1 Why was it important to compile the Buddha's teachings?
2 How did members of the Council show they agreed on the correct version of the teachings?
3 What does Theravada mean?
4 Who were the Mahasanghika?
5 Why did the Theravada and the Mahasanghika disagree?

Think About It

6 Is it important for religions to have rules? Who should decide on which rules to include. Who should be allowed to change them? Draw up a list of rules for all human beings to live by.

Question

• How accurate is the human memory? Look up feats of memory in the Guinness Book of Records.

The Emperor Asoka

Little is known about the history of Buddhism during the hundred years after the Second Council, but in 273 BCE, much of India was ruled by a man who was to change its destiny. The new emperor was called Asoka. He was the grandson of Chandragupta, an army officer who had driven the Greek forces from northwest India and founded the Indian Empire. Asoka continued to expand the Empire by force, but became more and more horrified by the slaughter of his bloody campaigns. He began to follow the Dharma and became an upasaka, a lay Buddhist who is committed to following the path but who is not a bhikku.

After this, Asoka's reign was characterised by a practical morality based on Buddhism: tolerance, non-violence, justice and respect. Indeed, he signed himself Priyadashin, which means 'The Humane One'. Despite the fact that Asoka allowed his subjects to practise any religion they chose, Buddhism flourished and rapidly became the established religion throughout his empire. As an upasaka, he became a man of peace, extending friendship to neighbouring countries in the name of the Dharma, and setting a noble example in the care he showed his subjects. He built hospitals, wells and reservoirs, providing much needed employment for his people.

He inscribed stones and pillars with 'Edicts', giving moral and religious guidelines. He built stupas to house relics of the Buddha, and marked places associated with events in the life of the Buddha with information pillars.

Asoka gave upasakas (lay Buddhists) the authority to maintain these religious places.

From some of Asoka's edicts:

"Everywhere provision has been made for two kinds of medical treatment, treatment for men and for animals. Medicinal herbs, suitable for men and animals have been imported and planted wherever they were not previously available"

"I have ordered banyan trees to be planted along roads to give shade to men and animals. I have ordered mango groves to be planted. I have ordered wells to be dug every half-kos [half mile] and I have ordered rest houses to be built."

"King Priyadashin wishes members of all faiths to live everywhere in his kindom."

"[Officers] are commissioned to work among the soldiers and their chiefs, the ascetics and householders, the poor and the aged, to secure the welfare and happiness and release from imprisonment of those devoted to Dharma. They are also commisioned to work among prisoners to distribute money to those who have many children, to secure the release of those who were instigated to crime by others, and to pardon those who are very aged."

"Twelve years after my coronation I ordered the following:

Everywhere in my dominions local, provincial and state officials shall make a tour of their districts every five years to proclaim the following precepts of Dharma: Obedience to mother and father; liberality to friends, acquaintances, relatives, priests and ascetics; abstention from killing living creatures; and moderation in acquiring possessions are all meritorious."

The bhikkus no longer had a monopoly on matters of faith.

During Asoka's reign, and under his authority, a Third Council of the Sangha was held at Pataliputra in about 250 BCE. It is likely that this Council was attended only by members of the Theravada tradition. This time, the Council succeeded in establishing the Pali Canon, the scriptures recognised by the Theravadins as being the exact teachings of the Buddha, although they were still not written down until about 100BCE.

Activities

Key Elements

1 By what name did Asoka like to be known?
2 What is an Upasaka?
3 In what ways did Asoka show his benevolent leadership?
4 How did Asoka communicate moral guidelines to his subjects?

The Three Yanas

As Buddhism spread, the many different groups of Buddhists moved outwards from India in different directions taking their particular traditions with them. Three different forms of Buddhism developed, called the three 'yanas'.

Hinayana (small vehicle) was a name used by the more progressive Buddhists to describe those who held very strictly to the monastic rules. This yana is represented today by Theravada Buddhism.

Mahayana (great vehicle) is used to describe the form of Buddhism represented by the more progressive monks at the Second Council. Mahayana Buddhists follow the same teachings as the Theravada, but have other scriptures and teachings as well.

Vajrayana (diamond vehicle) is the name given to a tradition which developed within the Mahayana. In Vajrayana Buddhism there are ceremonies and gestures which aim to help a person move more quickly towards enlightenment and which involve a person's emotions and imagination.

Definition

Yana means 'vehicle' - something which helps you to make progress along your path. It expresses the idea that Buddhist teaching is something a person can use to assist with his or her journey towards enlightenment.

I practise Theravada Buddhism. The teachings I follow are what the other two may call 'Hinayana'.

I practise Mahayana Buddhism, but I accept the Hinayana teachings as well.

I practise Vajrayana Buddhism. I accept the Hinayana and Mahayana teachings, but add some extra teachings and spiritual actions to them.

The Spread of Theravada Buddhism

One of the resolutions of the Third Council allowed the Emperor Asoka to send missionaries abroad to spread the Dharma. The most accessible route from India was by sea to the south. Tradition has it that Asoka sent his own son, Mahinda, to the country that is now called Sri Lanka at the invitation of its king in about 240 BCE.

So the Sangha grew in both size and vitality. It was in Sri Lanka that the Buddhist teachings and the rules for monks were first written down, forming what is known as the Pali Canon.

Mahinda taught the Dharma to the King of Sri Lanka and his courtiers, who readily accepted the new faith. Mahinda's sister, Sanghamitta, brought over as a gift a cutting from the original Bodhi tree under which Siddhartha became enightened. This cutting was planted in the capital city where it still grows today. It is probably the oldest plant in the world.

Other gifts followed, many of which were relics of the Buddha, including a tooth which is now a national treasure and is kept at the Temple of the Tooth at Kandy.

From Sri Lanka, missionaries were sent over the sea to Burma, and from there to Thailand. It was in these countries that Buddhism first

Inside the Temple of the Tooth, Kandy, Sri Lanka.

showed its great ability to adapt to local cultures, and it readily mixed with existing religious traditions. Theravada Buddhism is still the major religion in these countries today.

Activities

Key Elements

1 To which countries did Theravada Buddhism spread?

Think About It

2 Why do you think Buddhism spread so quickly?

3 Imagine you are Mahinda. How would you explain Buddhism to the people of Sri Lanka? What are the most important things to include? Is there anything you would leave out?

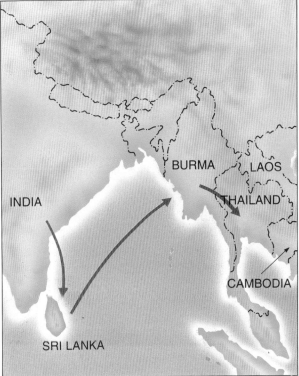

This map shows the early spread of Theravada Buddhism beyond India.

The Spread of Mahayana Buddhism

While Theravada Buddhism spread from India by the Southern Route, Mahayana Buddhism travelled northwards over the high desert plateaux of Central Asia. Mahayana Buddhists followed the same paths taken by nomadic peoples, military expeditions and traders. Consequently many staging and trading posts became towns of considerable religious importance, especially on the Silk Road to China. Many valuable religious texts have been discovered along this route.

From China, Buddhism moved to Korea which it reached in the latter half of the fourth century CE, and from Korea, it was introduced to Japan in the middle of the sixth century CE. As it spread, Buddhism took on a new, distinctive character as it adapted its teachings to suit the needs of the cultures in which it found itself.

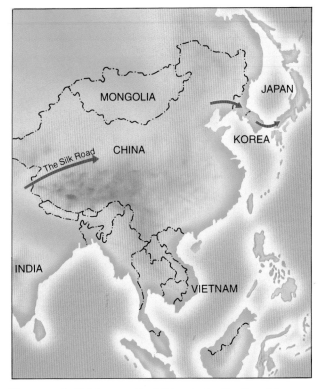

The spread of Mahayana Buddhism to the Far East. Vietnam has a mixture of Mahayana and Theravada.

The Spread of Vajrayana Buddhism

Vajrayana Buddhism developed in northern India but spread northwards to Nepal. In the 7th century CE it was introduced to Tibet by its King, Srongtsen Gampo. Two of his wives were Buddhists, one from China and one from Nepal, and between them, they taught him the Dharma and he accepted it, sending to India for Buddhist teachers to come to Tibet.

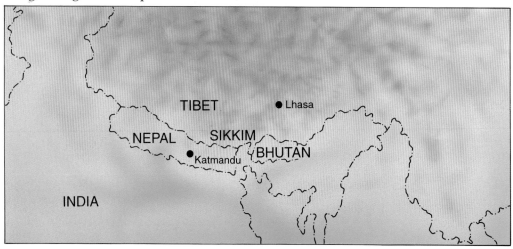

Countries to which the Vajrayana form of Buddhism spread.

Buddhism's Decline in India

Hinduism retained a very strong hold on the people in India, and the Brahmin priests opposed Buddhism. Many Hindus thought of the Buddha as one of the many appearance on earth of the Hindu god Vishnu, so there was no need to follow a specific Buddhist path.

The Buddhist Sangha became increasingly dominated by large universities and monasteries, rather cut off from the life of ordinary people. When Buddhism received the support of a ruler, it continued to flourish, but without that support the monastic centres could not survive.

Then, when the Muslims invaded Northern India, they destroyed the monasteries and killed thousands of monks. Nalanda, the largest of the monastic universities, had up to 40,000 students at any one time. When it was destroyed in 1197, it marked the end of Buddhism in India. But by then, of course - in its three different forms - Buddhism had already spread to South East Asia, the Far East and the Himalayas.

For many centuries, the places associated with the Buddha were controlled by Hindus. Nowadays, Buddhism is growing again in India, and places like Sarnath, shown above, are visited by Buddhists from all over the world.

Buddhist Missionaries

Although some lay believers, usually travelling traders, were responsible for the spread of Buddhism, most of this work was undertaken by bhikkus.

Having turned away from family life, the bhikkus were free from responsibilities and were therefore able to travel widely in order to teach the Dharma. Sometimes travelling was undertaken simply in order to teach the Dharma, but travelling was also seen as a goal in itself as it broadened their experience of life.

Sometimes bhikkus joined trading or military expeditions, while some travelled by invitation. When they arrived in foreign lands, they mixed with the same company as the expedition leaders - kings, princes and scholars - and so the people who first learned the Dharma were in a position to influence the whole nation.

Remember...

Buddhism was spread entirely by non-violent means, never by war. It was never the intention of the Sangha to convert people and so there was never any need to use force. Foreign powers were attracted to Buddhism partly because it came from countries of high culture, like India and China, but mainly because they saw its teachings to be common sense. In addition, of course, Buddhism was prepared to adapt many of the religious beliefs and customs which already existed.

Even though there have been disputes between different sects within the Sangha, violence has never been used as a means to resolve these conflicts. Disputes have traditionally been solved by discussion and debate. If this is not possible, Buddhists are content to live alongside those who follow different rules or teachings.

The Sangha Today

We have seen that as Buddhism spread from country to country it adapted according to the political, social and religious systems with which it came into contact. Because Buddhist missionaries originally spread the Dharma to foreign countries by appealing to state leaders, Buddhism has always had an important relationship with with politics and the state. Indeed, since Buddhists believe that the Dharma embraces every aspect of life, it is concerned with the secular world, too. A Mahayana sutra (teaching) states: "Education, politics, language and daily life are all part of the Dharma." (Lotus Sutra, ch.19). The modern Sangha comprises not only monastic Bhikkus, but also lay believers who take refuge in the Three Jewels.

Although travellers from Europe had come into contact with Buddhists in the East, it was not until the 19th century that much about Buddhism was known in the West.

During the 20th century, many Buddhists from traditionally Buddhist countries settled in the West and continued to practise their religion. Equally, Westerners became interested in Buddhism, and many new Buddhism communities were formed.

Just as Buddhism adapted itself in order to make the Dharma relevant to the people of Tibet, or China, so it has adapted itself to meet the needs of people in Western countries.

Discuss

"The Buddha's teachings were diluted when Buddhism adapted itself to local customs."

"The Buddha's teachings have remained pure, but they are presented to different people in different ways."

• Which of these statements do you agree with? Why?

Activities

Key Elements

1 List all the countries mentioned in this chapter to which Buddhism spread, and against each of them say which of the three forms of Buddhism are found there.

Think About It

2 Most Buddhists do not attempt to convert anyone, but are happy to explain the Dharma if asked. Do you think it is right to try to convert people?

Assignments

1 From what you already know about the Buddha's life, his teaching and his followers, answer the following:
- Why are monasteries important in Buddhism?
- Does a person have to be a monk or nun to be a true Buddhist?
(You may want to look back over your answers once you have considered the monastic Sangha again in chapters seven and nine.)

2 Make a short film of interviews with people answering the question 'Is it wrong to try to convert people to a religious belief?' At the end of the interviews, give your own summary.

4

Meditation and Worship

- Shakyamuni and Meditation
- Samatha Mediation
- Vipassana Meditation
- Chanting

- Zen
- Juzu
- Worship (Puja)
- Shrines (Butsudan)

Try to empty your mind of all thoughts. It's difficult, isn't it? The fact is that our minds are constantly filled with thoughts, flitting from one to another. Our minds are a confused jumble of ideas. And even if we do succeed in getting rid of those thoughts, we are still left thinking, 'I must stop thinking.'

One of the main aims of a follower of the Dharma is to see clearly, to be aware of life as it really is. In order to do this, he or she has to train the mind to be in control of the thoughts and ideas that fill it. Then thoughts motivated by greed, anger and ignorance can be discarded and replaced by thoughts of peace and tranquility. The Buddhist practice which encourages this is called Samatha meditation.

But people are controlled by what they feel as well as what they think. It is therefore important to cultivate positive emotions of good-will towards all, contentment and happiness. This happens as part of meditation, but it is also helped by worship, in which a person can express joy or gratitude, or admit to things that have gone wrong in life.

Meditation and worship may be enjoyable, but they are not ends in themselves. They are the means by which Buddhists seek to transform their lives. Their value depends on the way in which a person is able to allow the calmness and positive feelings that come through meditation to gradually influence the rest of his or her life.

Shakyamuni and Meditation

According to legends about Shakyamuni, the Buddha had a natural inclination to meditation and became highly skilled in its techniques at an early age.

One story tells of the young Prince attending an agricultural ceremony with his father. There he watched worms being eaten by small birds, and then those birds themselved being killed by larger birds of prey. He began to reflect on this experience, the impermanent nature of life and the causes of suffering, and this reflection turned into a deep meditation.

After he left the palace to lead a religious life, Shakyamuni was taught more advanced meditation techniques. He was trained in meditation on 'emptiness' (see a later Buddhist version of this idea on page 64) by Alara-Kalama and later was taught meditation which goes beyond perception and non-perception by Uddaka-Ramaputta. Whilst he easily reached the highest states of meditation under these two teachers, he nevertheless found that neither could bring him the enlightenment he sought.

Shakyamuni became enlightened after sitting in meditation under the Bodhi Tree. It is said that at this time he achieved even-mindedness, serenity and wisdom in which neither joy nor sorrow, happiness nor suffering are experienced. Having arisen from his meditation, Shakyamuni is said to have remained in this state for a week afterwards.

During the forty-five year period of ministry following his enlightenment, Shakyamuni is said to have practised seated meditation lasting anything from a few days to three months.

His disciples, the first bhikkhus, also practised meditation on a daily basis. Each twenty-four hours was divided into six periods of four hours, starting at sundown:

Period 1   in seated meditation.
Period 2   sleeping.
Period 3   seated meditation.
Period 4   washing, working, meditating and going out to to receive food.
Period 5   eating the food they had been given and then sitting in meditation to allow it to digest.
Period 6   was spend in meditation, hearing Shakyamuni teach, and discussing the dharma.

This may seem a very harsh routine to us today, but during Shakyamuni's time in India, meditation was very common. In fact, it was such an ordinary thing to do that no instructions on meditation were written down at that time: there was no need to explain them.

The Origins of Buddhist Meditation

Meditation in Buddhism is a form of Bhavana, or self-development. The origins of Bhavana go back to ancient Indian spiritual exercises called Yoga. Hindu Yoga consists of 8 stages:

1, 2   Making a conscious effort not to harm others and to establish good relations with them
3, 4   Sitting postures and control of the breath
5   Withdrawing the mind from external things and looking inwards.
6   Fixing the mind on a single object or thought
7, 8   Meditation, allowing the mind to rise above ordinary thought and be directly aware of reality.

These were taken up and developed by the Buddha. What Buddhists do when they meditate or worship may look very similar to the Hindu religion, but Buddhists do it in order to deepen the particular Buddhist view of life, which was outlined in Chapter 2.

Activities

1   Write up the episode of Shakyamuni at the agricultural festival as a children's story, with appropriate illustrations.
2   Write a diary entry for a day in the life of a bhikku or bhikkhuni at the time of Shakyamuni.

Samatha Meditation

In order to have control over the mind, it is helpful to have a subject on which to focus attention. Ideally the meditation subject would be one that suits the individual's character. For example, if we have tendencies towards greed and selfishness we might take death as a personal subject for meditation. Then we shall begin to see that everyone must die, both good and evil, rich and poor. We will realise that greed is futile in the face of death, and this will produce feelings of calm and dispassion in us.

However, one type of Samatha meditation that is suitable for everyone is that where the subject of concentration is our own breath.

Sit in a comfortable position, upright with legs uncrossed. Now close your eyes and concentrate on your breathing, becoming aware of breathing in and breathing out quite naturally through the nose. Don't try to regulate your breath, but just take full breaths, whether long or short. Slowly your mind will settle. If thoughts enter your mind you will find that they seem somehow weak and distant.

With practice, this type of meditation becomes easier. As you concentrate on breathing you come to realise the extent to which we depend on it for life. Breathing becomes more delicate, and it may even happen that breathing appears to stop altogether; mental activity becomes less and less, and peace and happiness will arise.

Walking Meditation

You don't have to be sitting down to calm the mind: you can do it while walking.

Find a place to walk without being disturbed - either to and fro along a straight line, or round in a circle. Walk naturally; become aware of the movement of your body; feel the ground beneath your feet and the air through which you pass. Let your mind settle into the whole experience of walking.

Activity

Draw three columns on a piece of paper. In the first column write down words which describe how you feel at this moment. Now try the Samatha exercises described on this page. First try sitting for about ten or fifteen minutes. Afterwards, write down words which describe how you felt **during** the exercise in the second column and **immediately afterwards** in the third. Compare the three lists. You may like to write a poem using the words you have written.

Alternatively, you could think of colours which you associate with your feelings and, perhaps, shapes. Use these colours and shapes to make an abstract piece of art which you feel represents your feelings.

Now show your work to someone else. Can they describe your feelings by looking at what you have drawn?

This is one of a number of different ways to sit for meditation. The important thing is to feel comfortable and relaxed, but also to be upright and alert.

The Brahma Viharas

Brahma Vihara means 'Sublime State' and by meditating upon the Brahma Viharas a person develops feelings of love, compassion, joy and peace towards all living things.

The four Sublime States are:

(i) **Metta** This is usually translated as 'loving kindness'. In meditating upon metta, a person first of all wishes himself of herself well (you cannot love others until you are also able to love yourself), and then spreads the positive and friendly thoughts outwards towards all other beings.

(ii) **Karuna** This means active compassion; understanding the nature of suffering and sharing the suffering of others.

(iii) **Mudita** This is sympathetic joy in which the meditator shares the happiness of all other beings.

(iv) **Upekkha** This is a state of peace and serenity, in which, with a well-balanced mind, a person looks on all beings - whether friendly or not - with the same positive attitude of care and well-wishing.

Meditating on the Brahma Viharas may take the form of a visualisation. In the case of Metta Bhavana, or Meditation on Love, you could try to visualise the spreading of love from yourself to you friends and acquaintances, to your community, and further on to the rest of the country and the whole world.

Alternatively, a passage of text could be taken as a subject of meditation. For example, in the case of Upekkha Bhavana, a suitable passage may be:

> A truly wise man will not be carried away by any of the Eight Winds: prosperity, decline, disgrace, honour, praise, censure, suffering and pleasure.

As far as the Brahma Viharas are concerned, thought is action. In other words, meditating on the spreading of love throughout the universe, for example, is itself the way to start spreading love throughout the universe.

In the 6th century CE, the Chinese Buddhist Chi-I wrote about the meditation on Metta like this:

> If, in a state of dhyana (meditation)... we practise realising the good qualities of other people, there will come a feeling of great compassion for all sentient life. In this connection we will have vision and recollections of our parents, our close kinsmen, our intimate friends, and our hearts will be filled wth inexpressible joy and graitude. Then there will develop similar visions of compassion for our common acquaintances, even for our enemies, and for all sentient beings in the five realms of existence. When we rise from our practice of dhyana after these experiences, our hearts will be full of joy and happiness and we will greet whoever we meet with kind and peaceful faces.

(from his Dhyana for Beginners)

Notice that Chi-I does not claim that meditation works some kind of magic - it is just that a person who has been meditating in this way will gradually come to treat people differently, will come to look on everyone with kindness and friendliness.

Discuss

- Do you think it is possible to treat everyone in a friendly way? How does meditation on the Brahma Viharas try to achieve this?
- In your own words, explain how this form of meditation works.

The effect of meditating of the Brahma Viharas is like ripples on the surface of water - gradually spreading outwards.

Vipassana Meditation

It is clear that you don't have to be a Buddhist to practise Samatha meditation. It is, more than anything, a way of relaxing and calming the mind. Vipassana meditation, on the other hand, is an important step on the path to enlightenment. In fact, it follows from the seventh step of the Noble Eightfold Path, Right Mindfulness, whereas Samatha relates to the sixth step, Right Effort.

Vipassana means insight. In other words it refers to a system of mental development that consists of looking inwards, looking at your mind as if you were an outside observer. In this way the meditator can break through the conventional workings of the mind to see things as they really are. Clearly, Vipassana meditation cannot be learnt from a book: it must be taught by a master. Only one who is skilled in meditation can pass on the techniques to pupils.

We are used to considering thoughts in relation to ourselves: the word 'think' must have a subject, a thinker. So we consider the thoughts that go through our minds to be **our** thoughts: 'I thought of that.' But if we are aware of the Three Marks of Conditioned Existence, then we see that there is no 'I' to do the thinking. The thinker and the thought are one and the same. It is like saying, 'The light flashed ' - the flashing is the light. When you realise this you are in Samadhi, the eighth step of the Noble Eightfold Path.

Samadhi is a state of very deep peace. It is deeper than the peace obtained from Samatha meditation because it continues at all times. On the other hand, Samatha is often practised in preparation for Vipassana. Samadhi is considered to be one step away from Nirvana - but that step is a large one.

Vipassana is usually practised in a sitting position, with legs crossed and the feet resting, soles upwards, on the thighs. The back should be perfectly straight, at 90 degrees to the legs. This is known as the Lotus Position. However, someone who is well practised in Vipassana will do it while sitting, walking, standing, or lying down. Vipassana is, after all, having a clear understanding of the workings of the mind, being aware of everything, and having clear understanding of every kind of action and movement: dressing, picking up a drink, eating, speaking, going to sleep.

> ### Fact Box
>
> Buddhists may use visual aids to help them meditate. A **Mandala** is a pattern showing features of enlightenment, drawn in a circle. Buddha images and mandalas are sometimes found on cloth wall hangings, called **Thankas**.
>
> Mandalas and Thankas are found especially in Tibetan Buddhism.

Activities

Key Elements

1 Explain Vipassana in your own words.

2 Explain Samadhi in your own words.

Think about it

3 Why do you think Samatha might be good preparation for Vipassana?

4 'The light flashed' is an example of a phrase where the subject (the light) and the predicate (flashed) are the same. Can you think of other examples?

5 Try sitting in the lotus position (or the easier cross-legged position shown on page 45). From what you know of Buddhism, why do you think it is called the 'lotus'?

Chanting

Many Buddhist traditions make use of sounds and words as an aid to meditation. A phrase used in this way is called a Mantra, and it is believed to have a mystical power if recited repeatedly. The Mantra is recited by chanting. Chanting is a bit like singing on one note. In order to do it properly, you should hum deeply through the nose and say the phrase at the same time.

One of the most famous mantras is **Om Mani Padme Hum** from the Tibetan tradition. It is very difficult to translate a mantra like this into English because each word means a lot more than just one English equivalent. Perhaps the simplest English expression is 'Hail to the Jewel of the Lotus'. However, the translation really isn't very significant; what is important is the sound that the mantra produces when chanted.

Another famous formula that is often chanted is the Tisarana, or the Three Refuges which we looked at in chapter three. Turn back to page 34 and you will find the Refuge formula written in Pali. Try chanting it. Remember to hum deeply through the nose while saying the words. Chant on your own first of all until you feel confident with the words. Notice particularly the rhythm of the phrases. Now try chanting in a group. Congregational worship is not common in Buddhism, but chanting is one example of it.

Activities

Key Elements
1 What is a mantra?
2 What is the most popular mantra in Tibetan Buddhism?

Think about it
3 Find out about how sound is produced and how it travels. How far do sound waves travel? Do they ever come to rest? What do sound waves do when no-one can hear them?

Kanjin

Kanjin means to observe your own mind, or to see the truth of your life. In this sense it could be described as a form of Vipassana. However, Kanjin is a method used in some Buddhist traditions, especially in Japan, which makes use of both chanting and a visual object of concentration.

Some of the Nichiren schools, for example, chant the phrase '**Nam Myoho Renge Kyo**'. Again, this is difficult to translate into English, but roughly it means, 'I dedicate my life to the mystical law of the universe (Dharma) and the law of cause and effect (Karma) for eternity'. In order to aid concentration, this is chanted to a paper scroll inscribed with Chinese and Sanskrit characters representing different aspects of life, including enlightenment. The scroll is called Gohonzon which means 'sacred object of worship'. Nichiren Buddhists believe that chanting to the Gohonzon will gradually bring them closer to enlightenment.

Sound is caused by vibration, and vibration is another meaning of the word 'kyo'. Sound vibrations can have very powerful effects: you may have seen how they can break glass, for example. Nichiren Buddhists believe that chanting 'Nam myoho renge kyo' sends vibrations throughout the world and beyond to bring enlightenment everywhere it goes.

Activities
- Write a list of different sounds (e.g. a waterfall, birds singing, a lion's roar). Beside each one write down how that sound makes you feel.
- Try chanting as a group (either the Tibetan or Nichiren chants). How did it make you feel?

I beg your pardon?
Be warned... Japanese Nichiren Buddhists often greet one another with 'Nam Myoho Renge Kyo' and may also answer the telephone in that way.

Zen

The word Zen is the Japanese equivalent of the Chinese Ch'an, meaning meditation. However, we have seen that many different schools of Buddhism place great emphasis on meditation as a means to enlightenment. All schools would agree that the only difference between a Buddha and an ordinary human being is that a Buddha is enlightened: in all other respects they are the same. In other words, all people have the capacity to be enlightened, just as all people have the capacity to be angry or sad.

Zen therefore says that enlightenment exists within all human beings all the time. The aim of Zen practice is to become aware of one's own enlightenment. This is called Satori. In the hustle and bustle of the modern world we have become obsessed with moving from one thing to another, with needing to know what will happen in the future. We do this so much that we rarely allow ourselves the opportunity to enjoy the present. One important aspect of meditation is that it enables us to sit still and do nothing. The aim of Zen practice, then, is not to try to become a Buddha or reveal one's Buddhahood in the future, but to see it now. It could be said that the aim of Zen is not to aim!

The meditation practice of Zen is called Za-zen, or sitting Zen. Sitting in the lotus position is very important, for it allows the meditator to breathe easily and slowly. He will put his hands into the dhyana-mudra (see page 111) and keep his eyes open. Remember: meditation is about being aware.

Zen considers there to be five kinds of meditative practices which go deeper and deeper.

1. Bompu is a very superficial form of meditation. Bompu means 'ordinary'.
2. Gedo refers especially to meditative practices of other religions. These practices may be useful, but do not lead to enlightenment. The word gedo means 'outside way'.
3. Shojo refers to Theravada meditation. Mahayana Buddhists often call Theravada 'Hinayana' or 'small vehicle'(see Chapter 3) because they do not consider it to be capable of leading all people to enlightenment. Shojo (also 'small vehicle') is used for the same reason.
4. Daijo is Japanese for Mahayana, or 'great vehicle', and refers to meditation which leads to enlightenment.
5. Saijojo is the purest form of daijo, the highest form of meditation.

In a Zen monastery, za-zen takes place in the Zendo, a hall used for meditation during the day and sleeping at night.

While the monks meditate, an attendant stands or walks up and down behind them carrying a large flat piece of wood like a paddle. If he sees a monk falling asleep or sitting badly, he will bow to him and then hit him across the shoulders with the paddle.

This is not seen as a punishment, but rather a way of helping the monk keep alert. It is debatable whether all monks see it this way!

The amount of time spent on za-zen varies according to the time of year. At certain times it goes on for sixteen hours at a stretch, interrupted occasionally for the monks to march around the floor to keep them alert.

It is possible for even za-zen to become so much a matter of routine that instead of helping the monk to reveal enlightenment, it may stand in his way. In this case, Zen employs a technique called Mondo, a kind of rapid question-answer that frees the mind from usual worldly thought. Another device is the Koan, a word or phrase that makes no logical sense, designed to take the mind above the level of ordinary thought. We shall look at these techniques in more detail in chapter eight.

Activities

Key Elements

1 What is the mantra of Nichiren Buddhists?
2 What is a Gohonzon?
3 What does Gohonzon mean?
4 What is satori?

5 What does za-zen mean?
6 Outline the five types of Zen meditation in your own words.

Juzu

Juzu (Mala in Sk) is the Japanese word for prayer beads which aid concentration during worship. For example, some people use them to count the number of times they have chanted a mantra. People did not use prayer beads at the time of Shakyamuni, and they were only introduced about a thousand years ago. Before that, people calculated the number of mantras by counting red beans. After their introduction, juzu became part of San'ne, or the 'Three Robes' carried at all times by Japanese bhikkus. (The other two are the surplice and the monk's robe.) Today they are also used by lay believers.

There are variations in the form juzu take in various sects, but there are common features. Juzu are a string of 108 beads, representing the 108 kinds of Bon-no, or worldly desires and the means of overcoming them. Each end of the string is placed over the middle finger of each hand; the hands are then put together with juzu in between. Some Buddhists cross the string to signify the denial of worldly desires.

Juzu usually have two tassels at each end to represent the Buddha and the Dharma. Some sects add a third tassel on the right-hand side to represent the Sangha.

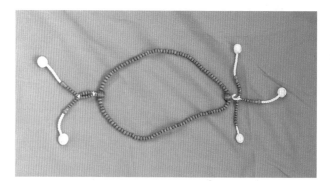

A Japanese-style juzu, and (below) a mala as used by Tibetan and other Buddhists.

Activities

Key elements

1 What are juzu?
2 Why are there 108 beads?
3 Why do some Buddhists cross the juzu?

Worship (Puja)

It may seem odd that Buddhists worship and make offerings when they do not believe in God.

They do not worship Shakyamuni Buddha as a god, for he was a human being - although of a very special kind, since they believe that he was fully enlightened. Also, Mahayana Buddhists think of him as one Buddha among many, and everyone as having a Buddha-nature.

Some Buddhists would say that Puja, the Sanskrit word for worship, is a way of involving the emotions in following the Buddhist path. It is also a natural expression of gratitude for someone who has felt the benefit of the practice of his or her religion.

Other Buddhists emphasise the idea that in worship they make offerings to the buddha-nature, the potential for enlightenment which they believe exists in all living things.

In Buddhism there are no rules about how or how often one should worship. Some Buddhists find it helpful to have a shrine at home and to have simple acts of worship each day. Others go to a temple to worship - some daily, some only at special festivals. When we look at the different forms of Buddhism, we shall see how each of them includes elements of worship.

A boy making an offering of incense at a shrine. This simple act of devotion to the Buddha is performed throughout the Buddhist world. Just as the smell of incense spreads out to fill a room, so good deeds are said to spread out to influence the world.

Emotions are important. Celebrating; saying 'thank you'; confessing faults; wishing someone well - Buddhist puja allows a person to do all these things in a simple and direct way. Puja does not work by magic, but it allows a person's emotions to come into harmony with their thoughts and actions.

During a puja, worshippers go up to the shrine to make their offerings, while others chant a mantra.

Setting up a shrine and thinking about what to put on it is an important part of worship.

Shrines (Butsudan)

Butsudan is a Japanese word which means literally 'place of the Buddha'. It is sometimes translated as 'altar', but this leads to an important misunderstanding about Buddhism. An altar is a place of sacrifice, and sacrifice has never played a part in Buddhist practice or Buddhist thought. At no time in the history of Buddhism has life been taken as an offering. The word 'shrine' is a better translation, because it implies that it is a place where something special is kept.

In all forms of Buddhism, ceremonies are held regularly in temples. However, lay Buddhists, particularly those of Mahayana sects, have shrines at home where they worship. The layout of the shrine and the objects associated with it vary from one branch of the Buddhist Sangha to another, but there are some common features.

There is usually a statue or picture of Shakyamuni or some other Buddha in the centre of the shrine. (On the other hand, it may be a symbolic diagram of enlightenment such as the Gohonzon of some of the Nichiren sects.) Mahayana shrines in particular are likely to have a whole variety of buddha images.

Shrines have other symbolic objects:

Vegetation. This will normally be flowers. The life of a flower is very short, and within a matter of days it will open up, bloom, fade, then shrivel and die. It will, however, leave seeds for regeneration. Some Buddhist sects prefer to use evergreen leaves on their butsudans. In either case, vegetation is a symbol of both impermanence (anicca) and eternity.

Water. India, the birthplace of Buddhism, is a very hot country in which water has always been a very valuable commodity. Offering water at the butsudan is therefore a symbol of respect and reverence.

Candles. Light is an important symbol in many religions. In Buddhism a candle flame lighting up the area around it is a conspicuous symbol of enlightenment.

Incense. The fragrance of incense pruifies the air. As the sweet-smelling smoke permeates

This shrine is in the village of Noyant, a small mining community in central France. In the 1950s refugees from Vietnam settled in the village and continued to practise Buddhism. Notice the offerings of flowers and fruit, the candles and the sticks of incense. The bell is on the floor to the left of the centre of the photograph.

the atmosphere it symbolises the Dharma being spread around the world.

Bell. Most Buddhist sects separate sections of their ceremonies by ringing a bell. This may be seen as a symbol of karma, the law of cause and effect: the harder you hit the bell, the louder it rings. The bell is often placed a cushion shaped like a lotus flower. The lotus is itself a symbol of cause and effect since it produces both seeds and flowers at the same time. This indicates the Buddhist belief that the effect of whatever you do is determined at the same time as you do it.

Food. Some Buddhists offer food at shrines.

Books. Most butsudan have copies of the texts of sutras which may be read or chanted.

Toba. Some Japanese Buddhist sects offer wooden tablets called toba as memorials to the dead.

Photographs. Sometimes they will be of those who have died. More often the photographs will be of Buddhist teachers.

A shrine is treated with great care and respect. It is usually cleaned every day, the water and food are changed daily, and the vegetation is changed regularly. Nothing is wasted: even the water can be re-used, perhaps to water a plant or even make a cup of tea.

Since the shrine is a symbol of the Buddha's body, the offerings made at it are also symbols of things necessary to sustain life: food, water, shelter, light and warmth. They can therefore be seen as objects to stimulate the five senses:-

Taste is stimulated by water and food.

Sight is stimulated by candle light.

Smell is stimulated by the fragrance of incense.

Hearing is stimulated by the sound of the bell.

Touch is stimlated by the use of juzu (prayer beads - see page 50).

There are many different kinds of shrine, from the very simple to the elaborate. See also the shrines on pages 11 (beneath the Bodhi Tree), 39, 81, 99 and 124.

Fact Box

Images on a shrine

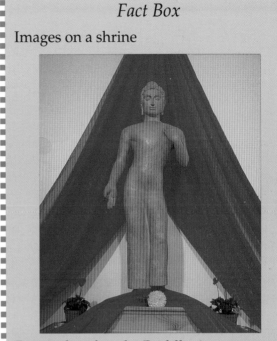

Remember that the Buddha is not seen as a god and is not worshipped. He is seen as an enlightened teacher, and as someone who shows what enlightenment is like. He is also seen as the source of compassion and wisdom.

Buddha images are visual aids. They express qualities of the Buddha. When a Buddhist makes an offering in front of a Buddha image, he or she is acknowledging the importance of what that image represents.

In chapters 8 and 9, we shall be looking at images that are used in the Mahayana and Tibetan traditions.

Activity

• Design a shrine. Remember that it should be respectful, but that does not mean that is cannot also be colourful and joyful. Buddhists believe that imagination and creativity are characteristics of the buddha-nature

Activities

Key elements

1 What does the word 'butsudan' mean?
2 Why should a butsudan not be called an altar?

3 What objects are usually found at a butsudan?
4 Whom do Buddhists worship?

Think About It

5 Do you have an object of worship? If so, what is it? Your bike? Your boy/girl friend? Your computer? Yourself? In what ways do you worship?

6 Look at the photograph of ripples on water (page 46). In what way does it ilustrate the effect of the Brahma Vihara meditations?

Assignments

1 Compose texts for meditation on each of the Brahma Viharas
2 Conduct a survey on people's feelings during mediation. Which words come up most often when people describe their feelings?
3 Make a video of your group meditating and chanting. Write a commentary to explain what you are doing and why to an audience that knows nothing of Buddhism.
4 What do you think 'worship' means? Brainstorm this word as a group and write a report on your conclusions.

5

Scriptures

- Vinaya Pitaka
- Sutta Pitaka
- Abhidhamma Pitaka
- Questions of King Milinda

- Classical Chinese: a crash course
- Mahayana Writings
- Tibetan Writings
- The Importance and Use of Scriptures

Like any good teacher, the Buddha suited his teachings to the capabilities of his listeners. His aim was to tell all people about the nature of life and how to avoid suffering. He would teach this in one way to dedicated monks and in another way to simple lay believers, so that everyone would be able to grasp his meaning at one level or another.

The monastic Sangha compiled the teachings of the Buddha after his death. The Rules of the Sangha (**Vinaya**) and the Buddha's sermons (**Sutta**) were at first recited in a language called Pali. Out of respect, these teachings were not written down for many centuries. In fact, the Pali language was a language only to be spoken - it did not have a written form. When it eventually came to be written down, it had to be written using alphabets from other languages.

As time passed, the circumstances of the teachings were forgotten, and the sermons became more difficult to understand fully. Later Buddhists had to interpret and explain the teachings. These explanations eventually formed a third section, the **Abhidhamma**, alongside the Vinaya and the Suttas. Abhidhamma means 'higher teaching'.

> ### Fact Box
> The earliest collection of Buddhist scriptures is known as the **Pali Canon**. The three sections of the canon (Vinaya, Sutta and Abhidhamma) became known as baskets (pitaka), so the Pali Canon is called the **Tipitaka** (Three Baskets).

An illustrated text from the Pali Canon.

After the Sangha split, each branch had its own version of the Tipitaka. Mahayana Buddhists used the ancient Indian language of Sanskrit for their scriptures.

As Buddhism spread, the canon was added to and translated into other languages. The languages used are not important; what counts is the ideas contained in the scriptures. In many cases, we only know scriptures through their later translations.

A long time elapsed before the Buddha's teachings were written down, and, although the monks took care in reciting the teachings and stories, changes may have crept in. Even though little of the Buddhist canon may contain the actual words of Siddhartha, most of the teachings can be traced back to him. In any case, Buddhists believe that any later additions were written by enlightened people who were expressing their Buddha nature.

Fact Box

Theravada Buddhists

... use the Tipitaka (in Pali) and some other early texts

Tibetan Buddhists

... accept both the Pali and the Sanskrit texts of the Theravada and the Mahayana, but add their own Tantric writings

Mahayana Buddhists

... accept the same Pali texts (but refer to them as the Tripitaka, the Sanskrit term), but add their own sutras, in Sanskrit.

Zen Buddhists

... claim that they have a tradition of teaching that comes down to them through their teachers direct from the Buddha.

Activities

Key Elements

1 What is a canon?
2 What does Tipitaka mean?
3 What are the three sections of Tipitaka?
4 Why was the Abhidhamma written?
5 Which school of Buddhism uses Pali?
6 Which language is used by the other school?
7 What is the difference between Tipitaka and Tripitaka?

Think About It

8 Why does it not matter to Buddhists that much of the Tipitaka is probably not an exact record of the actual words used by the Buddha? Do *you* think it matters?

Vinaya Pitaka

Vinaya means discipline, so the Vinaya Pitaka is often called the Book of Discipline. It contains the rules of behaviour that bhikkhus and bhikkhunis are expected to keep. Most of it is written in the form of reports of real cases which led to the formation each rule.

The Pali Vinaya is in three parts:-

(i) Sutta-vibhanga is concerned with the rules for bhikkhus and bhikkhunis, together with explanations and commentaries.

(ii) Khandhaka deals with the regulations for communal living (kamma-vacana), including rules about clothing and food.

(iii) Parivara contains extra precepts, and varies considerably from school to school.

The rules themselves are known as Patimokkha (P) or Pratimoksha (Sk). There are 227 altogether, and they are recited every two weeks in monasteries throughout the world.

Patimokkha means bond, and so these rules came about to ensure that individuals in the Sangha could live together in harmony. In this sense they are not rules to stop people from doing things, but rather they are guidelines to help bhikkhus and bhikkhunis become aware and mindful on the path to enlightenment.

Here is a selection of Patimokkha rules (actually taken from a Sanskrit version), starting with the most serious.

*"**Here are the rules about offences which deserve expulsion from the Sangha:-***

Sexual intercourse; taking anything which is not given; intentionally taking the life of a human being; claiming falsely spiritual achievements.

Here are the offences which deserve suspension from the Sangha:-

Four offences of sexual misconduct which do not result in intercourse; matchmaking; building a temporary or a permanent hut which involves the destruction of living beings; falsely accusing other bhikkhus; causing conflict, or taking the side of someone who causes conflict, in the Sangha; refusing to take punishment for breaking the rules.

Here are the rules which deserve forfeiting the right to share the Sangha's robes:-

Accepting silver or gold; buying articles with silver or gold; selling articles; keeping donations which were intended for the whole community.

Here are the rules which deserve an unfavourable rebirth:-

Lying; making fun of other bhikkhus; teaching the Dharma to a woman, unless an intelligent man is present; destroying vegetation; sitting alone with a woman in the open; asking for luxury foods when in good health; deliberately taking the life of an animal; drinking alcohol; having a chair or a bed made with legs higher than twenty centimetres."

Activities

Key Elements

1 What does Vinaya mean?
2 How many Patimokkha rules are there in the Pali Vinaya Pitaka?

3 What does Patimokkha mean?
4 Why do monks or nuns need rules for living in a vihara (monastery)?

Think About It

5 The Patimokkha rules are divided into sections according to the punishment which would result from the rule being broken. Would you move any rules to another section? Which ones? Why?

6 Keeping the same sections, write your own rules for a community of men and women.

7 Do you think the punishments are fair? Which ones are, and which are not?
8 Remember what you have learnt about karma. Ought a vihara punish a bhikkhu, or should it leave his fate to karma? Or is punishment the working out of his karma?

Sutta Pitaka

The word Sutta means 'thread', and indicates that just as thread runs through a piece of cloth to keep it whole, so each of the Buddha's teachings has a central theme which runs through it. The Sutta Pitaka, then, is a collection of myths, stories, sayings and teachings relating to the Buddha and his life.

The Sutta Pitaka is usually divided into five sections, or nikayas:-

(i) Digha-nikaya (Long Teachings) contains 34 suttas, including the Maha-parinibbana-sutta which describes the last three months of the Buddha's life and almost certainly records some of his actual words.

(ii) Majjhima-nikaya (Medium-length Teachings) contains 152 suttas grouped in fifteen 'vaggas' or sections.

(iii) Samyutta-nikaya (Grouped Teachings) contains 7,762 sutras in 56 groups, arranged roughly according to subject. This nikaya contains the Dhamma-cakka-pavattana-sutta, Buddha's first teaching after his enlightenment.

(iv) Anguttara-nikaya (Adding-one-each-time Teachings) contains 2,308 suttas arranged in eleven groups. The peculiar title of this nikaya derives from the fact that the first section deals with single items to do with Buddhism; the second section describes two kinds of Buddhas, two virtues of forest-living, and other 'double' items; the third section deals with the three sorts of bhikkhus and other 'triple' items; and so on up to eleven.

(v) Khuddaka-nikaya (Minor Teachings) contains fifteen suttas which do not readily fit into the other nikayas. This nikaya contains some of the most famous of the suttas, including the Dhammapada, the Metta-sutta on the meaning of love, and the Jataka stories.

Some of the teachings provide a practical guide to living. Here is an example from the Singalovada Sutta.

A child should honour his parents and do for them all that he is supposed to do. He should serve them, help them with their work, cherish the family ancestry, protect the family property, and hold memorial services after their deaths.

The parents should do five things for their children:

avoid doing evil, set an example of good deeds, give them an education, arrange for their marriage, and let them inherit the family wealth at a proper time. If the parents and child follow these rules, the family will always live in peace.

A pupil should always stand up when his teacher enters, wait upon him, follow his instructions well, not forget an offering for him, and listen respecfully to his teaching.

At the same time, a teacher should act rightly before a pupil and set a good example for him; he should correctly pass on to him the teaching he has learnt; he should use good methods and try to prepare the pupil for distinction; and he should not forget to protect the pupil from evil in every possible way. If a teacher and his pupil observe these rules, their association will move smoothly.

Question

• Do you think that one side should do things for the other only if the other keeps their side of the bargain? Why?

The most famous scripture in the Pali Canon is in the Sutta Pitaka, and is called the Dhammapada, or the Way of the Dhamma. The Dhammapada is a collection of 423 verses set in 26 vaggas, or chapters. It gives moral guidelines to those following the path to enightenement. Here are some examples.

'Hatred does not stop hatred. Only love stops it. This is an ancient law.

A fool who knows that he is a fool is, for that very reason, a wise man. A fool who thinks he is wise is a fool indeed.

An evil deed need not immediately cause trouble to the man who did it. But it catches up with the careless fool, just like fire smouldering in ashes.

As a cowherd with a stick drives his cattle to pasture, so old age and death drive us from life to life.

The one who protects his mind from greed, anger and stupidity is the one who enjoys real and lasting peace.

To utter pleasant words without putting them into practice is like having a fine flower without a fragrance.

An insincere and evil friend is more to be feared than a wild beast: a wild beast may wound your body, but an evil friend will wound your mind.

A spoon cannot taste of the food it carries. Likewise, a fool cannot become wise just by associating with wise men.

To conquer oneself is a greater victory than to conquer thousands in battle.

A great rock is not disturbed by the wind; similarly, the mind of a wise man is disturbed by neither honour nor abuse.

To live a single day and hear a good teaching is better than to live a hundred years without knowing such a teaching.

A friend who points out mistakes and imperfections and condemns evil is to be respected as if he has revealed the secret of hidden treasure.

Rust grows from iron and destroys it; so evil grows from the mind of man and destroys him.

The secret of health, both mental and physical, is not to mourn for the past, not to worry about the future, and not to anticipate troubles, but to live wisely and earnestly in the present.

Question

- Look through the verses from the Dhammapada. Which do you agree with most? Which least? Give reasons.

The Sutta Pitaka also contains the Jataka. This is a collection of 547 stories about previous lives of the Buddha, known as 'Birth Stories'. The stories illustrate moral points and emphasise the qualities a person needs if he or she is to make progress towards enlightenment. Here is an example:

Once there was a Prince who was skilled in the use of the five weapons. One day he was returning home from his practice when he met a monster whose skin was impenetrable.

The monster started for him, but nothing daunted the Prince. He shot an arrow at it, but the arrow fell useless. Then he threw his spear which failed to pierce the skin. Then he threw a bar and a javelin, but they failed to hurt the monster. Then he used his sword, but the sword broke.

Having used his five weapons, the Prince attacked the monster with his fists and his feet, but to no avail, for the monster clutched him in his giant arms and held him tight. The Prince even tried to use his head as a weapon, but in vain.

The monster said, "It is useless for you to resist; I am going to eat you."

But the Prince answered, "You may think I have used all my weapons and am helpless, but I still have one weapon left. If you eat me, I will destroy you from inside your stomach."

The Prince's courage disturbed the monster, who asked, "How are you going to do that?"

The Prince replied, "By the power of Truth."

The monster then released him and begged to be instructed in the Truth.

This fable teaches that disciples should persevere in their efforts and not give up in the face of setbacks.

Question

- The Jataka story gives a moral at the end. What other lessons can be learnt from it? (Hint: What if the monster is part of you that you want to change?)

Activities

Key Elements

1　What does Sutta mean?
2　What does 'Dhammapada' mean?
3　What is the Dhammapada?
4　What are the Jataka stories about?

Think About It

5　Look again at the extract from the Singalovada Sutta. Do you agree with the things children should do for parents? Do you agree with the things pupils should do for teachers?
6　Compile your own lists of five guidelines for behaviour for the following pairs: child / parents; pupil / teacher; husband / wife; brother / sister; boyfriend / girlfriend; friend / friend (same sex).
7　What reasons would a Buddhist give for following the guidelines of the Dhammapada?

Abhidhamma Pitaka

The Buddha taught specific people in specific circumstances according to their ability. Once these teachings were taken out of their context, they became difficult to understand. It became necessary to write commentaries on the Dhamma, and when these commentaries were collected together, they became the third 'basket' of the Tipitaka, the Abhidhamma Pitaka.

The Abhidhamma Pitaka contains seven separate works:-
(i)   Dhammasangani (Enumeration of Dhammas): an analysis of the Dhammas, including mental states.
(ii) Vibhanga (Distinctions): explanations, and questions and answers.
(iii) Puggalapannatti (Descriptions of Persons): an analysis of character types.
(iv) Kathavatthu (Subjects of Discussion): Buddhist philosophy.
(v)   Dhatukatha (Discussion of Elements): an examination of the elements of existence.
(vi) Yamaka (Book of Pairs): definitions of confusing terms.
(vii) Patthana (Book of Relations): details of how particular dhammas are related by 24 different links.

Since the different schools interpreted the Dhamma differently, their Abhidhammas are very different in details. All of them, however, try to explain the philosophy of Buddhism and describe the workings of the human mind in a way that we would call psychology.

Some of the Abhidhamma is very difficult to understand. Try this:

> *"None unconverted are ever found*
> *To dwell within the Pure Abodes,*
> *Nor those who in the holy life*
> *Are in the first or second path;*
>
> *No saints amongst those without perception*
> *Nor in the realms of punishment;*
> *But all may reach the other states,*
> *Be they within the paths or not."*

On the other hand, some of the Abhidhamma gives answers to questions that many Buddhists may have. This example settles the question of whether strong relationships can survive from lifetime to lifetime.

> *An old couple once came to the Buddha and said, "Lord, we were married having known each other throughout our childhood, and there has never been a cloud in our happiness. Please tell us if we can be married again in our next life?"*
> *The Buddha answered, "If you both have the same faith; if you both received the teaching in the same way; if you help others in the same way; and if you have the same wisdom, then you will have the same mind when you are reborn."*

Activities

Key Elements

1   What does Abhidhamma mean?
2   What is it about?

Think About It

3   Look back at the section of karma (in chapter 2). Buddhists believe that each person has his or her own karma. How might the Buddha have explained his suggestion that the old couple in the Abhidhamma share some aspects of their karma?

Questions Of King Milinda

Although it is not part of the Pali Canon, the Questions of King Milinda, the *Milinda-panha* (P), is a very important Buddhist work.

Milinda is the Pali version of the Greek name Menander, and King Menander was an Indian king of Greek ancestry. The book records a dialogue between the King and the Buddhist teacher Nagasena, in which the King asks questions about Buddhism and Nagasena answers them with great and convincing skill.

It was written about the middle of the second century BCE, though it is unlikely that it records an actual conversation. It was a way of making some Buddhist teachings clear at a time when many people were becoming confused.

In this extract, King Milinda wants to know about the Buddhist ideas on rebirth. If the body disintegrates at death and, if there is no soul, who or what is it that is reborn?

> "The King asked, 'When someone is reborn, Nagasena, is he the same as the one who just died, or is he another?'
>
> The Thera (senior monk) replied, 'He is neither the same nor another.'
>
> 'Give me an illustration.'
>
> 'When you were a new-born baby, were you then the same person as the one who is now grown up?'
>
> 'No. The baby was one thing, I am another.'
>
> 'If that is the case, then you, who are grown up, have had no mother, no father, no teaching and no schooling! Are we to conclude that there is one mother for the egg, another for the foetus, another for the baby, another for the man? Is the schoolboy one person and the person who has finished school another? Is the person who committed a crime different from the person who is punished for it?'
>
> 'Of course not! But what is your answer to all this?'
>
> 'If a man lit a lamp, would it shine throughout the night?'
>
> 'Yes, it would.'
>
> 'Is the flame which burns at the end of the night the same as the one that burns at the beginning?'
>
> 'No, it isn't.'
>
> 'Are we to conclude that there is more than one lamp, then?'
>
> 'No. The light shines throughout the night because of the one lamp.'
>
> 'Exactly. And this is what the dharma is like. At rebirth one dharma starts while another stops; but the two processes are continuous. The first consciousness of rebirth is not the same as the last consciousness of the previous existence, and yet it is not separate; just as you are not now a baby, but you are not a separate person from the baby you once were.'
>
> 'Can you give me another example?'
>
> 'If milk is left, it turns into curds, which turn into butter, which turns into ghee. Is the milk the same thing as the curds, the butter or the ghee?'
>
> 'No; but they have been produced because of it.'
>
> 'Exactly. And this is what a series of dharmas is like.'"

(In this passage, 'dharma' means 'thing'. See also the illustration of this teaching on page 28)

Activities

Key Elements

1 Who was King Milinda?
2 Who answered his questions?
3 Why was the Questions of King Milinda compiled?

Think About It

4 How would you answer Nagasena's question: are you the same person as you were when you were a baby?
5 What reasons would you give to support your answer?
6 Write the Buddhist ideas on rebirth in your own words.
7 Do you find Nagasena's arguments convincing?

Mahayana Writings

There is no fixed Mahayana canon, though different Mahayana traditions have arranged Buddhist texts in different languages: Sanskrit, Tibetan, Japanese and Chinese. The Chinese is the most famous. It contains:-

1. Tripitaka:
(i) Vinaya, which contains much of the Theravada rules.
(ii) Sutras, which are grouped like the first four Theravada nikayas. The groups are called Agamas. A fifth group consists of Jataka stories.
(iii) Abhidharma, which contains translations of some of the Theravada Abhidhamma as well as commentaries on Mahayana Sutras.

2. Sutras:
These translations of specifically Mahayana sutras are divided into sections:-
(i) The Lotus Sutra
(ii) Prajna-paramita sutras - Teachings on the Perfection of Wisdom.
(iii) The Avatamsaka Sutra - The Flower

Garland Teaching.
(iv) The Ratnakuta Sutra - The Jewel Teaching.
(v) The Maha-parinirvana Sutra - The Nirvana Sutra.
(vi) The Great Assembly Teachings
(vii) General Sutras
3. **Tantras:** these outline complicated meditation and visualisation practices
4. **Sastras:** treatises, or explanations of Mahayana schools.
5. **Commentaries:** on the sutras, vinaya and sastras.
6. **Histories and Biographies.**
7. **Encyclopaedias and Dictionaries.**

Altogether, the Chinese Canon comprises 2,184 texts in 55 volumes with a supplement of 45 volumes.

The Lotus Sutra

The Lotus Sutra is possibly the most important of the Mahayana sutras. In Japan, where it is very popular, it is known as *Myoho Renge Kyo*. Its Sanskrit title is *Saddharma-pundarika Sutra*, which means 'Sutra of the white lotus of the absolute truth'.

The message of the Sutra is that the Buddha nature is the basis of life, and that everyone is capable of becoming a Buddha.

But if everyone has an equal opportunity to become a Buddha, who was *the* Buddha? According to the Lotus Sutra, different Buddhas appear at different times in history to teach the Dharma. Shakyamuni was the Buddha for our particular world and time.

To illustrate difficult points and make it easier for ordinary people to understand, much of the Lotus Sutra is in the form of stories and parables.

For example, the Lotus Sutra says that the world is a place of suffering, but all human beings have access to the happiness of Buddhahood taught by the Buddha. Only their greed, hatred and ignorance (the Three Poisons) prevent them from realising it. The following story is told to illustrate this:

Suppose there was a very wise doctor who could cure any disease. He had many sons. One day he leaves the house to visit a patient far away.

While their father is away, the sons happen to take some medicine which poisons them. They cry out and writhe on the ground.

When the father returns home, he discovers that his sons have been poisoned, and, while some can still think clearly, others have lost their reason.

On seeing their father, the sons are overjoyed. They beg him, 'We are so happy to see you. We have been foolish enough to take poison by mistake. Please cure us and save our lives.'

Seeing his sons in such pain, the father mixes up a medicine. and gives it to them, saying, 'Take it and you will be cured of all your pains.'

Those sons who have not lost their senses notice that the medicine has outstanding colour, smell and taste. They immediately take it and are completely cured.

Those sons who have lost their senses are also pleased to see their father return, and ask him to cure them. But when the father offers them the medicine, they refuse to take it. The poison entering their systems has made them lose their reason and they think the medicine will be useless.

The father thinks to himself, 'My poor sons have lost their minds and so will not take the medicine that will cure them. I must think of a way to get them to take it.'

So he says, 'I have to go away again. I am travelling a long way and I am old. Consider that I may never come back. I will therefore leave the medicine for you.'

The father then leaves. Later he sends a message home that he is dead.

When the sons hear of their father's death, they are broken hearted. In their grief, they come to their senses and realise the truth. They take the medicine and are cured immediately.

On hearing that his sons are cured, the father returns home and makes himself known.

Activity

In the story of the wise doctor, what do the following represent: the Doctor; his sons; the poison; pain; the medicine; the sons who lost their reason; the sons who kept their reason; the 'death' of the father; the father's return?

Write down the meaning of the story in your own words.

Classical Chinese: A Crash Course

Many of the Mahayana scriptures were originally compiled in the Sanskrit language and translated into Chinese. In some cases, the Chinese translations are all that have survived. However, these translations are so faithful to the originals that they have taken on an importance of their own, and some Buddhists prefer them to the Sanskrit originals.

In this section we are going to look at the ancient Chinese language of some of the Mahayana sutras.

In Chinese, words are written in the form of characters rather than letters. In English, each sound we make can be represented by a letter or combination of letters. We have an alphabet of just 26 letters, and by combining these letters in various ways, we are able to write hundreds of thousands of different words.

But in Chinese each word is represented by a different character, and each character must be learnt. You can imagine that only very well educated people are able to read even a newspaper.

However, learning the characters is made easier if you know that many of these characters started life as simple pictures. If you recognise the picture, you can read the character. Chinese characters are used in Japanese, too, although they are pronounced differently, and today may have different meanings. Let's look at some examples.

The character for the word 'sun' was originally written ☉ a simple picture of the sun travelling around the earth. (What's wrong with this?) When woodblock printing was invented, it was found difficult to carve circles into the hard wood, and the charcter changed into a square shape 日. This character is still used today. In Chinese it is pronounced 'jih'; in Japanese, 'ni'.

Similarly, the character for 'tree' started life as 朩. In time it changed into 木. In order to convey the idea of 'root, source, place of growth', a line was drawn to represent the ground with a root below it 本 : 'land'. In Chinese, this is pronounced 'pen', in Japanese, 'hon'.

Let's put the two characters together:

日本 = Nihon (Japanese) = Jih-pen (Chinese)

You can now see where our word 'Japan' comes from, why it means 'The Land Of The Rising Sun', and why the Japanese word for Japan is Nihon (sometimes written Nippon).

Characters which started as pictures are called pictographs. Here are some more. Cover up the English translations and see if you can work out what they mean. Then try to explain why they have this meaning.

一	one	中	middle
二	two	門	door
三	three	舍	house
人	man	雨	rain
山	mountain	東	east

Here is a sentence from the Lotus Sutra. Underneath is written the classical Japanese pronunciation and the English translation. Cover up the English. Which character do you recognise?

| 其 | 智慧 | 門。 | 難解 | 難入。 |
| Go | chi-e | mon | nange | nannyû |

The door to wisdom is difficult to open and difficult to enter.

The Chinese character for 'not' is 弗 . It represents two bows which, when tied together, have their force neutralised. We have already seen that the character for 'man' is 人 . When it is combined with another character to make a new one, it is written 亻 .

The character 佛 means 'Buddha'. What does it mean literally? And what might this tell you about Mahayana beliefs about the Buddha?

The Prajna-paramita Sutras

Prajna-paramita means the Perfection of Wisdom, the final stage of spiritual perfection before enlightenment.

The Prajna-paramita Sutras are a collection of sutras on the subject of Buddhist wisdom compiled at the beginning of the first century BCE. Among the collection is the *Ashtasahasrika Sutra*, the 'Teaching in 8,000 Lines'. Over the next couple of centuries, this work grew to about 100,000 lines, but at the end of the fourth century CE two shorter versions were compiled. The first is the *Vajracchedika* (the Diamond Sutra) and the second is the *Hridaya* (the Heart Sutra).

So what is the Wisdom explained in the Prajna-paramita Sutras? Re-read the section on the Self on page 26. Here is another example to illustrate **anatta**.

What is a bike? Take it apart to find out. What have you got? Wheels, pedals, handlebars, frame brakes, cables, gears... but where is the bike?

Let's take this further. Take any one of these parts, say, a wheel:

What is a wheel? A tyre, a rim, spokes. Now, where is the wheel?

The point is that everything can be analysed into other parts, and each of those parts can be analysed... and so on. Buddhism concludes from this that nothing has any substance of its own, and therefore that everything is empty. The word Buddhists use for this emptiness is sunyata; to describe things as sunya is to say that they are empty.

So there really is no point in relying on anything or anyone to make you happy, since everything and everyone are sunya. In fact, clinging to empty things can only bring about unhappiness (dukkha).

This is what the Heart Sutra means when it says:

'Form is not different from emptiness; emptiness is not different from form. Form is precisely emptiness; emptiness is precisely form.'

Now, all this may sound rather negative and gloomy. But let's look at it the other way round. If everything is sunya, then nothing can tie us down: we are totally free. And this freedom is

Buddhahood. In the words of the Heart Sutra:-

'Complete emptiness (sunyata) is the foundation of Buddhahood. All those who become Buddhas in the past, present and future are fully awake to the perfect enlightenment because they have relied on the perfection of wisdom.'

So the wisdom of the Prajna-paramita Sutras is the realization that everything is sunya, and therefore everything has the Buddha nautre.

Activities

Key Elements

1 What does Prajna-paramita mean?
2 What are the short versions of the Ashtasahasrika Sutra called?
3 What does sunyata mean?

Think About It

4 Why do you think the Diamond Sutra is so called?
5 Why do you think the Heart Sutra is so called?
6 As a class, brainstorm the word Emptiness. Then write a poem using the word emptiness in a way that reflects what you have discussed.

Fact Box

Look back at page 20. Everything arises in dependence upon conditions. Nothing exists in a way that is independent of everything else. This is called *anatta* (no-self) and it is the starting point of the whole Buddhist way of looking at life.

The Mahayana idea of *sunyata* expresses the same idea. Everything is empty of its own existence; everything is part of everything else; you are part of the world, and you are free.

Tibetan Writings

Much of the Tibetan Canon consists of texts which are in the Chinese Canon. But there is material which is unique to Tibetan Buddhism, and more is being added all the time.

The Tibetan Canon is in two parts:-

1. bKa'gyur (pronounced Kangyur) which means 'Translation of the Word of the Buddha'.
(i)   Vinaya (monastic discipline)
(ii) Prajna-paramita Sutras
(iii) The Avatamsaka Sutra (Flower Garland Teaching)
(iv) The Ratnakuta Sutra (The Jewel Teaching)
(v)   Other Sutras (three-quarters Mahayana)
(vi) Tantras (texts on meditational practices)

2. bStan'gyur (pronounced Tengyur) which means 'Translation of Teachings'.
(i)   Stotras (hymns of praise)
(ii) Commentaries on the Tantras
(iii) Other Commentaries and Abhidharmas

Tantra

Part of the canon which is very important to Tibetan Buddhism is the Tantra. 'Tantra' means 'pattern', and refers to meditation techniques which involve visualisation. The meditator tries to cleanse himself spiritually and fill himself with fresh life-force. His vision transforms his mind and his view of the world around him. He may even take on different sounds and voices. The practices described in the Tantras are impossible to understand without a proper interpretation. You need to be given the key to unlock their secrets by a Tantric master.

Here are some examples of Tantric writings. From Going For Refuge:

I arise from my bed and wash myself; I sit with my face to the south. And I am in a cemetery, surrounded by dancing skeletons and a host of evil spirits, for they are the passions of the world.

And I fix my heart upon my hope of benefit and joy for all beings:-

I take refuge in the best of men, and in the peaceful Law...and in my master...and in my mind where emptiness and compassion are one...

And I awaken myself to enlightenment...: I firmly grasp the disciplines of virtue and take my vow to save

Tibetan scriptures are often written up on flags and displayed at festivals.

all beings: for I shall save the unsaved, and I shall encourage the weary, and I shall lead all beings to nirvana.

From The Four Immeasurable Contemplations

SRI-HERUKA! And I myself become the Blessed Cakrasamvara, Father and Mother, and from my mouth issues forth:-

A A I I U U R R L L A AI O AU AM AH KA KHA GA GHA NA CA CHA JA JHA NA TA THA DA DHA NA TA THA DA DHA NA PA PHA BA BHA MA YA RA LA VA SA SA SA SA HA KSA HUM HUM PHAT PHAT!

And from these syllables there radiates an immeasurable brilliance of white and red light: and it serves the aims of all beings, and it is gathered back and fills all the places of my body."

Activities

Key Elements

1 What does Tantra mean?
2 What are Tantras used for?

Think About It

3 Why do you think Tantric practices have to be taught by a master?
4 We often use sounds rather than words to express ourselves. What do the following express? Wow!, Ah!, Aaagggghhhhh!, Mmm!, Er.
5 What state do the Tantric syllables written above express?

The Importance and Use of Scriptures

Studying the Buddhist texts is one of the most important religious activities, for it is in this way that Buddhists learn about their religion. Of course, the bhikkhus usually have more time than lay believers for study, and so their function is to interpret the teachings and pass them on to others. However, in the light of karma, any form of meaningful contact with Buddhist texts will bring about positive effects. Therefore even hearing the scriptures being read will bring good fortune.

The Lotus Sutra emphasises what a rare opportunity it is to discover the Sutra in what are known as the Six Difficult and Nine Easy Acts. The six difficult acts are: to tell others of the Lotus Sutra, to copy it, to recite it, to teach it to even one person, to hear of it and enquire about its meaning, and to believe in it. They are said to be infinitely more difficult that the nine easy acts, which include walking across a burning prairie carrying a bundle of hay on one's back without being burned, or kicking a galaxy across the universe with one's toe! Teaching, studying or listening to the scriptures is therefore a source of good karma.

Most Buddhist sects use specific texts to recite in worship. Recitation by chanting is a traditional form of worship in Buddhism, and many Buddhists chant lengthy texts as well as mantras, sometimes several times a day.

Some Buddhist sects consider that chanting just the title of a text is sufficient. Nichiren, a mediaeval Japanese priest wrote:-

> 'Included within the word 'Japan' is all that is within the country's sixty-six provinces: all of the people and animals, the rice paddies and other fields...Similarly, included within the title of the Lotus Sutra is the entire sutra consisting of all eight volumes, twenty-eight chapters and 69,384 characters without exception...Chanting the title twice is the same as reading the entire sutra twice, one hundred titles equal one hundred readings of the sutra, and a thousand titles, a thousand readings of the sutra.'

In some Buddhist traditions, especially the Tibetan, books of texts are considered to be sacred, even more so than statues and images, since they contain the Dharma. They are therefore kept in places of honour in shrines and butsudans, the oldest copies having the places of greatest honour.

Activity

List the books that are special to you. Why are they special? How do you treat them? (Some people will not even bend the spines of books.) Where do you keep them?

Activities

Think About It

1 Look again at the Six Difficult and the examples of the Nine Easy Acts. What other 'Easy Acts' can you think of to compare with a rarity of finding and understanding the sutra?

2 Find out where the word 'shrine' comes from and what it originally meant. What does this tell you about the importance of Buddhist scriptures to Buddhists?

Assignments

1. Dramatise one of the Buddhist stories you have looked at (the Wise Doctor; The Prince and the Monster from the Jataka stories).

2. Calligraphy is a highly skilled art-form in China and Japan. Practise painting some Chinese characters with a brush and black ink or paint.

6

Ethics and Daily Life

- The 5 Precepts
- The Paramitas
- Family Life

- Monastic Life
- Social Action
- Getting rid of the Ego

People follow the Buddhist path in three ways:
- the way of morality
- the way of meditation
- the way of wisdom.

All three are important if someone is to make progress towards enlightenment and avoid the three poisons: hatred, greed and ignorance.

We have already looked at some of the meditation techniques used by Buddhists in order to develop calmness and insight. We have also seen some of the teachings of the Buddha, which are believed to lead to wisdom. But a person is unlikely to make progress in meditation or wisdom without a basis in morality.

In the 2nd century BCE, King Menander conquered part of the North West of India. He was interested in the Buddhist religion, and we have a record of a set of questions he put to the Buddhist sage Nagasena.

Nagasena explains the place of morality in the Buddhist life like this:

Just as vegetable and animal life grows in dependence upon the earth, so do the qualities of the Buddhist life (faith, enthusiasm, mindfulness, concentration and wisdom) grow and mature on the ground of ethics.

Just as an architect clears and levels the ground before he can build a town, so a person wanting to develop these qualities of mind should prepare himself by ethical integrity.

Living in the right way, with the right values, treating people in a morally responsible manner - these are not an optional extra, but essential as a basis upon which all the rest of the Buddhist path can develop.

In this chapter we shall look at the general principles by which Buddhists seek to live - principles which follow naturally from the Buddhist way of looking at life and which can be used in order to assist a person to develop.

When it comes to particular issues and lifestyles, it is impossible to generalise about how Buddhists live, or their daily routine. A monk in Thailand, a Japanese businessman, a Tibetan married lama, a member of the Western Buddhist Order working as a member of a 'right livelihood' team, a married person with family responsibilities and an ordinary job - each of these will have his or her own particular way of following the Buddhist path, and their responsibilities will be quite different.

The Five Precepts (Pansil)

Basic to the Buddhist way of life are the Five Precepts - principles of training. They are not absolute rules to be obeyed, but guidelines for how to behave in a way that will enable a person to make progress on the spiritual path, to develop good karma and avoid bad karma (see chapter 2).

> ## Discussion
> Do people have to lead 'good lives' to be religious?

A person becomes a Buddhist by 'going for refuge' to the Buddha, the Dharma and the Sangha and by accepting these five precepts. Buddhists often recite these precepts when they meet together as a way of re-affirming their commitment.

There are two ways of looking at the precepts. The more usual way is to see them as a list of things to be avoided. On the other hand, it is equally possible to list them in terms of positive qualities that a person should develop. Here we have the negative form, followed by the positive.

1. I undertake to abstain from taking life

This precept is against killing or harming living things - including animals. Because of this precept, many Buddhists are vegetarian. Some Buddhists argue that it is also 'taking life' if you deliberately do something to hurt or humiliate another person - you are, in effect, making out that their life is of little worth, which may make them feel depressed, depriving them of the enjoyment of life.

By deeds of loving kindness I purify my body (i.e. my life)

This attitude of loving and caring for all life is encouraged by the Metta Bhavana meditation (see chapter 5).

2. I undertake to abstain from taking what is not freely given

In its simplest form this is the precept against stealing. But it can be far more than that. You might do something which is quite legal, but which aims to exploit others for your own financial gain - that would also be against this second precept. Some forms of advertising might be seen as the attempt to take what is not freely given. It is not simply as matter of law, but an attitude that seeks to get what belongs to others, by whatever means. It can also be taken to apply to deliberately wasting the time of another person - stealing their time and their energy.

With open-handed generosity I purify my body.

In other words, I cleanse myself from all meanness and grabbing at what is not mine through cultivating at attitude of open-handed generosity, freely wanting all other creatures to do well. In this way, being generous benefits others *and* yourself.

3. I undertake to abstain from the misuse of the senses

This precept is against over-indulgence. In its simplest and most obvious form it is against sexual misconduct that harms oneself or others. Some Buddhists undertake to live without sex, so that they can follow the spiritual path in a more undistracted way. For others there are no strict sexual rules about how they should express their sexuality. The important point is that causing harm - either physically or emotionally - or taking advantage of another person sexually, leads to unhappiness and therefore is to be avoided. Some Buddhists extend this precept to include any form of over-indulgence e.g. in food or drink.

With stillness, simplicity and contentment I purify my body.

For a balanced life - a middle way between the extremes of luxury and hardship - it is important to be able to accept what you need, to be simple in what you want and to be content with what you have. For most Buddhists who are not monks or nuns, this means living in a simple by healthy way. There is no reason why a person should not enjoy sex, food, or new clothes, but it would be unhelpful for these to become the most important things in life.

4. I undertake to abstain from wrong speech

A Buddhist should avoid lying, slander, gossip, harsh speech and idle chatter.

With truthful communication, I purify my speech.

This involves being honest with other people and with oneself. It includes not giving the wrong impression, or 'putting on an act', but being yourself and sharing your thoughts in a straightforward way. Buddhist should also try to cultivate, helpful, gentle and kindly speech.

5. I undertake to abstain from taking drugs and alcohol which cloud the mind

Although some Buddhists do drink alcohol, they should to do so only in moderation and not allow their minds to become fogged and clouded by it. Some people mistakenly think that drink or drugs will help them escape from unhappiness, but that is not the Buddhist way of dealing with life.

With mindfulness, clear and radiant, I purify my mind.

Buddhism is about being 'awake'; a Buddha is fully awake to the truth of life. A person cannot hope to make progress if he or she tries to hide away from the truth by retreating into a drunken haze. We saw in chapter five that one of the purposes of Buddhist meditation was to help a person become more mindful - to be aware of everything that he or she does at every moment; to avoid going through life in a dream.

Mindfulness

An example of clouding the mind:
Someone who is anxious at a party may be tempted to take too much drink, in order to forget his or her anxieties and pretend that he or she is happy and confident. The trouble is that such a person may look more of a fool if he or she becomes drunk, and will have done nothing to help understand why he or she was anxious in the first place, or to do anything to change it.

For Buddhists, mindfulness should be cultivated all the time, not just in moment when extra skill is needed. Buddhists tend to say that anything which numbs the mind, which stops a person seeing and feeling what is happening, should be avoided. There are the obvious things - alcohol and drugs, for example - to avoid. But other things, including some games, interests, and forms of work will numb the mind, so that a person thinks of nothing else, or is clouded and dull. In the example given above, the party (which could have given the person an chance to enjoy friendship, to learn more about himself and to overcome anxiety) was an opportunity wasted.

Activities

Key Elements

1 What are the Five Precepts?
2 What are the positive qualities that Buddhists seek to develop as they keep the Five Precepts.

Think About It

3 Precepts are not the same as laws of the land. Make a list of actions which go against the Five Precepts, but which are not against the law.
4 Give examples of things that 'numb the mind'. Include at least one form of work, and one social activity, but exclude drink and drugs.

The Paramitas

The precepts are common to all Buddhists, but Mahayana Buddhists also speak of trying to cultivate the Six Paramitas - 'perfections' or qualities of an enlightened mind. These are the qualities that a person needs to develop if he or she is to make progress towards enlightenment.

Giving (dana)

This is the positive side of the second precept. A person who is generous shows that he or she is not grasping and craving for money or other goods, but is happy to let them go for the benefit of others. Many Buddhists emphasise that generosity is not simply a matter of giving money, but of giving time and skills for the benefit of others.

In some parts of the Buddhist world, dana is expressed especially in supporting those who are monks and nuns, so that they can be free from the need to earn a living, and can devote themselves to practising and teaching the Dharma.

Morality (sila)

We have already looked at the precepts which guide morality. A sense of morality - acting rightly towards other people as well as yourself, is an essential feature of the Buddhist life. If someone lives thoughtlessly, it is difficult to see how he or she could develop any of the other perfections.

Energy (virya)

It is not enough to think positive thoughts: Buddhists may need to take action in order to get things done. Showing loving kindness towards all creatures is not easy, nor is it much use if it is only a nice feeling. The Buddhist path may need carefully directed effort. Meditation can help with this; when people have definite goals to work towards, rather than minds that are scattered and easily distracted, they find that they have far more energy. Virya is the name Buddhists give to this energy that is directed towards doing good.

Patience (kshanti)

This does not mean always giving way to what other people want, but behaving in a thoughtful way, recognising everyone's different abilities and needs. You can only be patient with other people when you are patient with yourself - when you accept and understand your own abilities and limitations.

Meditation (samadhi)

We saw earlier that Meditation is important for the Buddhist way of life. If a person's mind is always rushing from one thought to the next, he or she is unlikely to be able to stand back and see life calmly, or to recognise what are the most important things.

Wisdom (prajna)

The basic teachings of the Buddha, especially the three universal truths - that everything changes, that things do not have a permanent fixed identity, and that life, because of these changes, is always going to involve some suffering - can lead a person to look at life honestly. Wisdom is not the same thing as book-learning; wisdom is seeing the truth of things and responding to them in a skilful and appropriate way.

Skilful Means (upaya kausala)

The problem with rules is that no two people are exactly the same; what is right for one person may be wrong for another. But the precepts and the paramitas are not rules, they are pointers to the sort of life that enables people to be healthy, happy individuals.

A wise person, guided by these pointers, will know what to do in each particular situation, but this takes skill rather than simple obedience to a rule. For Buddhists, the intention behind an action is most important. They hope to have the wisdom to act skilfully.

For this reason, Buddhists speak of actions as skilful or unskilful, rather than as good or bad.

Activities

Key Elements

1 What does paramita mean?

2 What are the Six Paramitas?

Think About It

3 Write down a practical example of each of these paramitas, and how it might benefit someone. Then write down in your own words how you think a Buddhist would describe it, and relate it to the Buddhist way of life.

4 Write down examples of actions which are right for one person but not another?

5 What problems might a Buddhist encounter trying to follow the Five Precepts while using skilful means? (Think about 'white lies' for example.)

Householders and monks...

Siddhartha left the family life and set out on his spiritual quest as a 'sadhu' (see page 10). Some of his followers took the same step, 'going forth' from family life to become wandering preachers. Later these wanderers settled to live in their viharas (resting places) and became monks or nuns.

Since most Buddhist scriptures or books on Buddhism are written by or for monks and nuns, it can appear that they alone are 'real' Buddhists. In practice, however, the majority of Buddhists are householders and even those who take monastic vows do not necessarily do so for the whole of their lives.

Under 'Family Life' we will look at ethical issues that apply to all Buddhists but especially those in the 'ordinary' world of work and families, under 'Monastic Life' we will look at the special rules that apply to monks and nuns.

Family life

In the *Mahamangala Sutta*, the Buddha lists things that lead to happiness and blessing. They include:

• not to associate with fools, but with the wise
• to live in a congenial environment
• a good all-round education and appreciation of the Arts

• highly trained discipline and pleasant speech
• supporting one's father and mother
• loving one's wife (or husband) and children
• having a peaceful occupation
• being generous and having a sense of duty
• helping relatives and acting blamelessly
• abstaining from evil and from intoxicating drinks
• reverence, humility, contentment, gratitude and listening to the Dharma

These are the application to ordinary family life of the Precepts and the Paramitas. They give an idea of the ideal life for a lay Buddhist.

There are no fixed ceremonies used by all Buddhists to mark the big events of family life - birth, marriage and death. Different countries have different customs. Issues of morality and lifestyle are considered by applying the precepts and using 'skilful means' to know what should be done in each situation.

Marriage and divorce

• Buddhists think of marriage as a personal matter between the people concerned rather than a religious event, although in some traditionally Buddhist countries a couple may go to their local temple for a blessing after their marriage has been registered.

• In Buddhist terms, there is no difference between a marriage and a couple who choose to live together. What matters is the quality of the relationship, not its legal status.

• As shown in the list above, Buddhists hope

that a marriage will be loving, but if the relationship breaks down, they accept divorce.
• In looking at the quality of a relationship, Buddhists may consider the first precept (Are the partners draining one another of life, or helping one another to live fully?), the third precept (Is the relationship based on sexual neediness or exploitation?) and the fourth precept (Are the couple honest and open with one another?).

Sex

• Sex is neither good nor bad in itself, but - like everything else - it may be used either skilfully or unskilfully. The fifth precept is against the unskilful use of sex: sex which harms, exploits or is based on dishonesty.
• Sex is a very powerful human drive; the potential for hurting or being hurt through sexual craving is great. Buddhists may seek to cultivate stillness, simplicity and contentment in order to establish a balance in their lives.
• Any form of craving makes a person dependent on the thing for which he or she craves. Some Buddhists - including those who become monks or nuns - choose to live without sex and find that this gives them greater freedom and makes spiritual development easier.
• Although some traditional Buddhist groups see heterosexual relationships as the norm, other Buddhists make no distinction between heterosexual and homosexual partnerships. What matters is not the sexual acts that a couple practise, but the quality of their relationship.

Death

• Buddhists generally cremate those who have died. Sometimes their ashes are put in a small stupa (see pages 86 and 114 for larger stupas) which is placed on a shrine. Larger stupas are built as a memorial to more important teachers. Photographs of those who have died are sometimes displayed on shrines.
• Before the cremation, some Buddhists may take the body to a shrine room and meditate in the presence of the coffin. It is a powerful reminder that we all have to face death at some time - that all things change and that there is no permanent self.

• Tibetan Buddhists in particular, think that after death a person passes through a state called the Bardo before being reborn (see page 117). During the weeks following the death, friends and family will meditate and wish the person well as they pass through the Bardo - sending them positive metta (see page 46) to help them on their way.

Food

• Following the first precept, Buddhists try to avoid taking life. Many Buddhists are vegetarian. Some are vegan - avoiding cheese, milk or any other animal product, on the grounds that these are the products of the human exploitation of animals.
• Where it is necessary on grounds of health, Buddhists generally eat fish or meat, since they have a duty to take care of their physical bodies. (You need to show compassion towards yourself as well as other living beings.)
• In the Theravada tradition, monks and nuns depend for their food on the gifts of lay people. They are expected to eat whatever is given to them, even if that includes meat or fish. Following the same principle, many lay Buddhists will accept these things if they are offered them and there is no vegetarian alternative. As with all these issues, there are no fixed rules, just general guidelines.
• Giving food is a good way to show generosity (dana). Lay people who provide monks or nuns with food regard this as a privilege and as a source of merit, or good fortune (see page 80).

Work

• To live by the precepts, a Buddhist will need to think carefully about the work he or she chooses to do, avoiding any activity which involves taking life or exploiting people.
• 'Right Livelihood' - one of the steps of the Noble Eightfold path, is used to describe any means of earning a living which conforms to Buddhist ethical principles.

Abortion and Euthanasia

• Buddhists believe that a new life starts at the

The way in which a business is run and the friendships that develop between those who work together, can be important. Some Buddhists therefore choose to work together in businesses that run on the Buddhist principle of 'right livelihood'.

This healthfood shop is one of three team-based right livelihood businesses run by the Croydon Buddhist Centre. Following the precepts, in order to be 'right livelihood', it has to be run in an ethical way, neither exploiting its customers nor those who work in it. Selling vegetarian food is compatible with the precepts and profits go to help the work of the Centre.

moment of conception. Abortion therefore involves the destruction of a life, which is against the first precept.

• An abortion is likely to have painful consequences - perhaps in terms of regret about what has been done, or a hardening of a person's attitude towards life. Sometimes, however, an abortion is suggested because allowing the child to be born would involve even greater suffering. There are no absolute rules in Buddhist ethics - sometimes a painful decision has to be made, and those who make it have to be prepared to accept the consequences.

• Euthanasia involves the destruction of life, but may seem the only way to avoid further suffering. Buddhists support the provision of nursing and medical care to allow a person to come to the end of his or her life in as painless and comfortable way as possible, and to help it to be a time of reflection and learning for both the dying person and his or her relatives. This is seen as a very positive alternative to euthanasia.

• Although it goes against the first precept, in certain very extreme circumstances suicide may not always regarded as unskilful, if it is done in full awareness and is the only way to avoid further suffering. In general, however, any taking of life, including one's own, is regarded as very serious and unskilful.

These are just some aspects of the Buddhist life and moral issues to which the precepts may be applied. It should be stressed that the central act of the Buddhist life is 'going for refuge' to the Buddha, the Dharma and the Sangha; the way in which a Buddhist lives should reflect that commitment, although no two people will do so in exactly the same way.

It is also important to keep in mind that, for Buddhists, there are no fixed rules to obey. You simply try to see what is the right thing to do in each situation, using the precepts as your guide. Although Buddhists may regret things that they have done, they should not feel guilty, but simply recognise their limitations and try to learn to act more skilfully in the future.

Activities

Think About It

1 Buddhism does not see marriage in religious terms; it is concerned only with relationships and the effect they have on individuals. Do you agree with this view? Do you think marriage should be marked by a religious ceremony?

2 Make two lists: one of jobs you think would not be suitable for Buddhists, and the other of those that would be particularly good for them.

3 Do you think there is a difference between killing an animal yourself for meat and eating meat which has been killed my someone else? Give reasons for your answer.

4 Making mistakes is something you learn from, not something to feel guilty about. How might this Buddhist attitude be put into practice? Give examples.

Monastic Ethics

Some Buddhists choose to become monks or nuns, not because there is anything wrong with family life as such, but because they want to be free from domestic responsibilities and distractions. This step should not be taken for selfish reasons, but in order to be free to explore and teach the Dharma to others.

Monks or nuns are expected to follow the five precepts (see pages 68 and 69), but add the following:

6. To refrain from eating after midday. Human beings need to eat in order to live, but a bhikku whose mind is occupied with thoughts of supper is making very slow progress towards Buddhahood!

7. To refrain from dancing, singing and watching unsuitable entertainments. Enjoyment of such things increases a person's worldly attachment. Bhikkus are not against entertainment and would not wish to stop anyone else from enjoying things. It is their personal decision to refrain from them.

8. To refrain from using scents or garlands. The Dharma is life itself, the reality in everything. You cannot improve on life by making it smell better!

9. To refrain from sleeping on high or broad (in other words, luxurious) beds. A bhikku should not think of sleep as an enjoyable pastime, but as a necessity. He can become enlightened only when awake and alert. Most Bhikkus sleep on a thin mat which they roll up during the day to carry with them.

10. To refrain from handling gold and silver. A bhikku should not be attached to worldly things.

Monks and nuns are celibate; in other words, they live without sex. This is because sex can be the most powerful of human cravings and is incompatible with the sort of life that monks and nuns have chosen to lead. In place of the third precept (not to misuse sex) they undertake to practise *brahmacharya*. This word means 'to live like the gods' - in other words, to be free from thinking of yourself as either a man or a woman and to relate to other people without allowing sex to get in the way.

There are many other detailed rules in the monastic 'vinaya' and monks meet regularly to recite them (see page 84). These are rules, rather than precepts, and their purpose is to ensure the smooth running of the monastic sangha and to create for all its members the right atmosphere in which to develop the qualities of the Buddhist life so that they can then go out to help others and preach the Dharma.

If a person fails to keep the more important rules - for example, by having sex - he or she would be asked to leave the monastic Sangha. For lesser offences a person may be suspended for a fixed period of time. Other things are left to karma - in other words, if you do something unskilful, you will be the poorer for it.

Equally, a person may choose to leave the monastic Sangha. There is no shame in wanting to do this and a person may enter and leave it up to seven times in the course of his or her life. Buddhists do not take vows for life - they may accept the monastic discipline in order to benefit from what it has to offer, and later may decide that the time has come to leave the order, marry and have a family. In countries where Theravada Buddhism is practised, there it is traditional for young men to enter a monastery for a short period (see page 83).

Monks and women

Some of the rules for monks may seem rather restricting. For example, no monk was allowed to teach a woman on her own. But in practice it was to avoid any situation where misunderstanding or temptation might occur, and to make sure that there was no opportunity for accusations of improper behaviour to be made against the Sangha.

There was also a danger that men and women might distract one another and some monks were worried about having anything to do with women. The Buddha's advice to his monks was to avoid contact with women as far as possible and to remain very 'mindful' and aware of themselves when they were dealing with them. Such advice simply reflected the practical problems of avoiding temptation.

Anagarikas

The Anagarika Movement was started in Sri Lanka by Dharmapala (1865-1933). An anagarika is half-way between a monk and a lay person, wears white robes and combines the spirituality of the monk or nun with the practical living in the world of the lay person.

Those who are to go for full monastic ordination generally spend two years as an anagarika first. Although anagarikas keep many of the monastic rules, they are allowed to handle money, which makes them particularly helpful to monks, since they can deal with the financial side of their needs.

Rules for nuns

The Buddha set down eight rules specially for nuns:

1 a nun, even if long experienced, should always pay respect to a monk, even one newly ordained
2 nuns should spend the rainy season retreats along with the monks, not on their own
3 every two weeks the nuns should wait for a monk to preach and conduct the special day during which the rules are recited etc. (see page 84)
4 at the end of the rains retreat, each nun should allow her conduct to be examined before the community of both monks and nuns
5 a nun who does wrong should do what is required of her by way of penance, and before the community of both monks and nuns
6 a nun may ask for full ordination after she has kept the rules for two seasons
7 a nun shall not abuse or reprove a monk
8 nuns may not speak in a company of monks, but monks may speak to nuns

These are severe, but were laid down in order to stop any nuns claiming superiority over monks. This may sound sexist, but the Buddha may have been concerned to prevent women from entering the Sangha for the sake of gaining social status. If they entered, accepting that they would be subordinate to the monks (as would happen in the rest of society then between men and women) then he would be sure that they wanted to be ordained for the right reasons, not for the wrong ones.

There are altogether 311 rules for nuns.

We all depend on others for the things we need. The monk with his offering bowl is a symbol of this. He will happily accept whatever his is offered by way of food and other necessities. He will also freely give people what he can - by teaching them the Dharma, by setting a good example and by offering then friendship and advice.

Activities

Key Elements

1 Why do some Buddhists choose to enter the monastic sangha?
2 Why are Buddhists allowed to leave and re-enter the monastic life?

Think About It

3 What do you think Buddhists mean when they say that sexual activity can be a 'selfish craving'? (Clue: remember 'anatta')
4 Why are rules for monks and nuns stricter than those for lay people?
5 Would it be more difficult for a lay person to keep the extra five precepts than a monk or nun? Why?

Social Action

On one occasion, the Buddha is said to have refused to preach until a poor, hungry peasant was fed. His followers too may therefore need to take social action.

Buddhism is sometimes wrongly described as an other-worldly religion, concerned to help people escape from the world and find their personal Nirvana. Such a Buddhism would be unlikely to do anything to challenge the way society works.

In fact, in the East, Buddhism has been challenging and changing society for two and a half thousand years. From the Emperor Asoka onwards, society has been influenced by Buddhist values. Here are some modern examples:

- During the Vietnam war, groups of Buddhists helped to develop local communities in places that had been ravaged by the war. They did not take sides in the conflict, but showed compassion towards those whose lives had been shattered by it.
- When there was civil unrest in Burma in the 1980s, Buddhist monks used non-violent means to help the political struggle. They organised demonstrations, held the weapons of army deserters in safe keeping, and their monasteries provided safe havens from those who were in danger of their lives.
- The Dalai Lama travels the world talking about Buddhism. But he also talks about the people of Tibet and the suffering of the people under Chinese rule. In this sense, he is politically active. He is seen by Tibetans as a practical and political as well as a spiritual leader and guide.

Like all religions, there have been times when Buddhism has been more active in changing society, and others when it has tended to accept the political situation in which it found itself.

'Engaged Buddhism'

Buddhist ethics is based on getting rid of the three poisons - greed, hatred and ignorance. This can apply on a personal level, but many Buddhists argue that it applied in a wider sense to the institutions by which our society operates. Thinking about the arms industry, or the profits made at the expense of people or the environment by multinational corporations, may be a way of seeing how the three poisons can operate across the world.

Tich Nhat Hahn, a Buddhist from Vietnam, speaks of 'engaged Buddhism' - Buddhism which is concerned about people and the way they live, and is engaged in trying to improve life for them. He sees it as a matter of bringing Buddhist values and spiritual qualities into all of life. He runs workshops to help people do just that - to develop kindness, to breathe mindfully under all circumstances and to live in a way that reflects basic Buddhist ethical principles.

There are many ways in which Buddhists are engaged. In Britain, for example, there is the 'Network of Engaged Buddhists' which is involved in a range of social issues. Buddhists are concerned with those who are dying, with the poor and homeless and with those in prison. Through the Karuna Trust, the Friends of the Western Buddhist order is particularly concerned to help the ex-untouchable Buddhists in India.

The Dalai Lama sometimes speaks of 'universal responsibility'. You can think of it this way:

- the world has limited resources
- the world has an increasing population
- the environment affects everyone, and what we do affects the environment

In everything that we do - choosing how to travel, what we eat, what sort of work we do, how we treat the environment - we have an effect on the rest of the world. Having a 'universal responsibility' means taking this into account. A person's karma (actions) always have consequences. Sometimes these are consequences for the individual person, but at other times they affect many others. To generate good karma therefore helps everyone, not just oneself.

How do you deal with the world's problems, whilst keeping the sense of peace that Buddhism seeks to offer? When he received the Nobel Peace Prize in 1989, the Dalai Lama said this:

..if you have inner peace, the external problems do not affect your deep sense of peace and tranquillity. In that state of mind you can deal with situations with calmness and reason, while keeping your inner happiness.

In other words, a person in a state of panic will achieve less that a person who is calm and has inner happiness. In this way there is really no conflict between developing inner spiritual qualities and social action. The first gives the deep inner security which makes the latter possible.

Care of the environment

In Buddhism, nothing has a fixed self; nothing exists separately from the conditions that bring it about. Therefore humankind is not separate from the rest of nature. In looking after the world around us, we are also looking after ourselves. Japanese Buddhists sometimes speak of *esho funi* - the unity of all living things.

Many of the ideas and precepts in this chapter can be applied to environmental issues.

Dr Ambhedka

Dr Bhimrao Ramji Ambhedka (1891-1956) was born an 'untouchable', outside the Indian caste system and shunned by those who considered that they were superior by birth.

He was determined to succeed and to overcome the limitations which kept most outcastes in poverty. He worked astoundingly hard at school and became qualified to go to college. He received help to continue his education and later studied in England and the USA, receiving a Ph.D in Law.

In spite of this, his untouchability made life very difficult for him when he returned to India. Nevertheless, he became greatly respected as a lawyer and politician and was involved in drawing up India's new constitution when the British handed over control. He became India's first Law Minister.

He continued to be particularly concerned about those who, like him, were 'untouchable' and who suffered, although 'untouchability' had been declared illegal.

He studied all the world religions, recognising that these 'untouchables' would need some new spiritual basis for their lives if they were to escape from their poverty and gain their self-respect. As long as they remained Hindu, they would suffer from the caste system. He finally became a Buddhist in 1956, along with 5,000 of his followers, but died a few weeks later.

Today there are millions of ex-untouchable Buddhists in India. They have great personal respect and devotion for Dr Ambhedka - often setting his photograph alongside images of the Buddha on their shrines. For them, he shows the Buddhist qualities of compassion, courage, energy and great determination.

Activities

Think About It

1 Some people say that Buddhism is a selfish religion. Why might they think that? Do you agree? Give reasons.

2 Why would a Buddhist be pacifist?

3 The Dalai Lama says that it is possible to be happy while dealing with world problems. From what you know about Buddhism, what do you think he means by happiness?

Getting rid of the Ego

Buddhism teaches that people are basically good and pure, but this purity may be covered over with layers of greed, hatred and ignorance. By avoiding these three poisons, and by trying to cultivate positive qualities, a person can allow their natural goodness to emerge. One way of expressing this idea is to say that all creatures have a Buddha-nature, and that all are capable of enlightenment.

The problem is that, if you get the idea that you are pure and on your way to becoming a Buddha, you may become self-centred. This is exactly the opposite of Buddhist teaching.

Buddhism says that the idea of a fixed, separate identity (an Ego) is an illusion. You are changing all the time. The molecules that make up your body (nourished by the food and oxygen you take in) are part of a wider physical world. Your thoughts come from others, and are shared with them. You cannot separate yourself from the rest of the world.

To be happy, a person needs to be free from grasping, attachment and guilt. Buddhists see these as coming from a false idea of the self: 'What's in it for ME? Why should I do what others want? It doesn't affect ME if others suffer!'

Getting rid of this false idea of yourself, and recognising that you are a small and constantly changing part of a massive universe, is likely to make you more concerned with those things that benefit the whole of life, not just yourself.

Some Buddhist mediation techniques are designed to help a person get away from this self-centred idea of the self, or Ego.

Questions

- Why is it important for a Buddhist to get rid of the Ego?
- Look at the five precepts (pages 68 and 69). How might an ego-less attitude help one to follow them? Give examples.

Assignments

1 Imagine a scene of conflict within a family (for example, a son or daughter who wants to stay late at a party, and a parent who forbids it). Now use the same scenario to write a play about what would happen in a Buddhist family. (Hint: What would they be thinking? How would they argue? Which precepts would they need to consider?)

2 During the rainy season, nuns must hold their retreat along with the monks. This is partly to make it easier for them to be celibate, assuming problems and misunderstandings are more likely to occur if the sexes are kept apart. Think of reasons why some schools are single-sex while others are mixed (co-educational). Hold a class debate: 'This house believes that all schools should be co-educational.'

3 Find out about the meanings of guilt and sin in different religions. Write an essay on this and why you think Buddhists do not believe in them. (There are no Buddhist words for either sin or guilt.)

4 The precepts offer guidelines for how people should treat one another, but they also apply to the way in which humankind treats the environment. Look through all the moral guidelines that have been set out in this chapter and see which of them can apply to the environment. Then write an essay on the care of the environment, using Buddhist ideas and values as a basis for saying what would be the most skilful way to treat the world.

7

Theravada Buddhism

- Distinctive Ideas
- Worship
- The Monastic Sangha

- Images of the Buddha
- Buildings
- Festivals

The monastic life is very important in Theravada Buddhism. Monks and lay people work to support one another. This boy is having his head shaved in preparation for the ceremony in which he will become a monk - not for life, but for a period of study and self-discipline. It is a sign that he is ready to take responsibility for himself and for his own spiritual development.

Distinctive Ideas

Since the Buddha taught different people in different ways, it is hardly surprising that after his death his disciples divided themselves into a number of groups. Each of these groups had slightly different ideas about the philosophy of Buddhism, though each was based on the Buddha's teachings.

Of those original groups, only one has survived to this day: the Theravada. The basic teachings of the Theravada school are outlined in Chapter Two, but in this chapter we shall look at some of the teachings which separate Theravada from the school which split from it, the Mahayana.

Wherever Buddhism is practised it takes on the culture and traditions of its host country. Theravada Buddhism is practised largely in Thailand, Burma and Sri Lanka. In each of these countries it has absorbed local customs, and so is practised slightly differently. In this section we shall look at some of the teachings which are common to all shades of Theravada.

At the heart of Theravada Buddhism lie the Three Marks of Conditioned Existence and the Four Noble Truths (see pages 20 - 23). These imply that all life is liable to suffering, and that the Buddhist path is the way to escape from a life of suffering and, perhaps after many lifetimes of practice, to achieve Nibbana (P).

According to the Theravada tradition, a person who becomes enlightened during his or her lifetime is called an Arahat. The word 'Arahat' means 'worthy of respect'. An Arahat is someone who has completed the Noble Eightfold Path; destroyed attachment or greed (tanha, see page 22), hatred and delusion; and has overcome dukkha.

It is very difficult to become an Arahat, but it would be far easier for a bhikkhu to become one than a lay person because the lay person cannot devote as much time as a bhikkhu to spiritual training. So Theravada Buddhism stresses the importance of life in a monastery (a vihara), and encourages every male to enter one for at least some time. In this way, they have a sporting chance of becoming an arahat.

Of course, in order to become an arahat it is important to lead a moral life so that you generate good or positive karma.

What is 'good' for one person to do in a particular situation may not be 'good' for another, so a Buddhist will try to do whatever is most appropriate, or 'skilful' in each situation.

A skilful act is sometimes called 'punna', which means 'fortunate', since it will bring good fortune. In English, punna is usually called 'merit'. There are three kinds of action which are punna:-
    1. Moral conduct (sila).
    2. Meditation (bhavana).
    3. Giving (dana).

Any act of giving will attract good fortune. However, the amount of good fortune you will receive depends largely on your motive for giving. Therefore it is considered particularly fortunate to give to make someone else happy. It is considered less fortunate to give hoping to get something back, or simply to gain merit.

The problem is that it would seem that rich people, or at least people with a lot of things to give, have a greater opportunity of building up a store of merit. However, the motive for giving is seen to be so important that it is possible to gain merit simply by rejoicing at someone else's act of giving.

In this way it is possible to enable others to receive the good fortune destined for you by tranferring your merit to someone else. Better still, the transfer of merit is itself punna! The transfer of merit is particularly important when someone has died. At this occasion, the family and friends of the deceased transfer merit to him or her and so encourage a fortunate rebirth. This is done at the funeral, seven days after death, and at anniversaries.

Lay people can gain merit by giving donations to bhikkhus. By giving in this way they can also transfer the merit to a deceased relative. And whilst a boy will gain merit by becoming a samanera or a bhikkhu, his mother will share this merit with him.

The three kinds of action which gain merit include ten particular actions:-
1 Gifts to arahats
2 The observance of the five precepts
3 Meditation
4 Making offerings at shrines
5 Caring for the sick and encouraging the good
6 Making gifts to a vihara with the purpose of benefiting deceased relatives and friends
7 Sharing merit with others.
8 Hearing Dhamma
9 Teaching Dhamma
10 Correcting one's perception of life

Activities

Key Elements

1 What is the aim of Theravada Buddhism?
2 What is an arahat?
3 Why is it difficult for a lay believer to become an arahat?
4 What is punna?
5 Why do Buddhists 'transfer merit'?

Think About It

6 Do you have something which reminds you of a special person or occasions? What is it? What does it remind you of? (e.g. A ring which belonged to your grandmother. Do you think it has a 'power' to bring your grandmother alive in your mind?)

Worship

Here the monks and nuns sit on opposite sides of the shrineroom, facing one another. It is quite usual for a shrineroom to be arranged in this way; it allows people to come forward during the worship to make their offerings before the shrine.

Worship may take place either at home or in the temple. No lay believer is obliged to visit a temple, although most of them do, even if only irregularly. Most lay believers will have their own shrine at home.

The bhikkhus worship in the shrine and meditation rooms of their vihara, usually once in the morning and once in the evening. Lay believers attend whenever they can, preferably once a day in Theravadin countries, otherwise on special occasions. There is no special time for attendance: there are no 'services' as such. Central to Theravadin philosophy is that each individual has to work out his or her salvation on his or her own. The bhikkus are there to give guidance and clarify the Dhamma, but that is all.

Acts of worship are important from a karmic point of view. Since every thought, word or action will have an effect, it is important to perform acts which will gain merit. Acts of worship fall into this category, since all thoughts, words and actions are performed for the Three Treasures. Offerings are therefore very important. Lay believers offer flowers, incense, candle light and food before an image of the Buddha. They also chant the Three Refuges and Five Precepts in Pali as an offering

or 'puja'. The recitation itself is called 'Pansil'. (See page 34 for information on the Refuges and pages 68 and 69 for the Precepts.)

Worship usually ends with a determination to transfer the merit gained through worshipping for the benefit of all beings:

May all beings always live happily
Free from enmity
May all share in the blessings
Springing from the good I have done.

Questions

- From what you know about Buddhism so far, explain what a Buddhist might mean by transferring the merit gained in worship.
- What effect do you think transferring merit has on the person who is worshipping?

Activity

Compose a closing prayer for a Theravada ceremony.

The Monastic Sangha

Originally, the Buddha and his monks travelled around, meeting together during the rainy season. As time went on, buildings were given to the monks for use when they met together, and these gradually became permanent monasteries (called viharas) where the monks lived all year.

A person may choose to become a bhikku and enter a vihara in order to remove himself from the sources of craving, to destroy attachment to desires and so attain enlightenment.

Although the Sangha is often thought of as the community of bhikkus, it really refers to all followers of the Dhamma. There is no doubt that the bhikkus could not survive without the support of lay believers who provide them with alms: food and donations of money. On the other hand, lay believers consider that they can create good or fortunate karma by contributing to the bhikkus and the life of the vihara.

However, the vihara serves the community in many ways, too. It acts as a community centre and a school, where the bhikkus not only teach children how to read and write, but they also teach adults how to build, farm and dig wells. It has the function of a bank, as lay people may use it to deposit valuable belongings for safe-keeping; and sometimes it is a hotel for lay believers to stay in when attending religious festivals.

Buddhists believe that an enlightened human being can affect his or her surroundings, just as a flame lights up all the space around it. So a vihara is considered to benefit all who live around it. As a result, lay people feel honoured to support the bhikkus in any way they can. On the other hand, if a bhikku behaves dishonourably it is the lay Buddhists who will drive him away!

Young men often join the Sangha for a short period of training and self-discipline. Some boys as young as seven are able to join as novice (trainee) monks.

Spending some time as a monk is thought to encourage self-discipline, and it is also believed to bring merit for both the young man himself and also his family.

In order to be admitted to the Sangha, a man must be healthy, unattached, and free from debt. As a symbol that he has given up his attachments to the world, he may walk around the vihara throwing coins at a crowd of lay believers. Young boys have a special meal with the monks before being dressed up as princes, like the young Siddhartha, and led on horseback around the vihara. Although they are being trained in the Dhamma, there is plenty of time for play and fun, and they see their parents often.

When a man is first admitted to the Sangha, he is known as a samanera, or novice. After some study he will be ordained as a bhikku. A few bhikkus may go on to become theras (Elders), and very few theras may go on to become mahatheras.

> ## Question
>
> • What do you think Mahathera means? Clue: Split the word in two: Maha (Mahayana?) and Thera (Theravada?).

On admission the samanera will shave his head and face, and put on the robes of the vihara. The robes consist of three pieces of cloth sewn together as rags may be, as a symbol of poverty. They are made from the cheapest cotton and are usually yellow, the colour of saffron. At this point he will take the Ten Precepts, or undertakings.

The Ten Precepts are not rules. They are really promises which the bhikku makes to himself, ideals he wants to live up to. The first five make up a moral code for all Buddhists to live by, even lay Buddhists, and the last five give guidance on how best to live as a Bhikku.

(See pages 74 and 75 for the precepts and rules that apply to monks and nuns.)

Life in a monastery offers a balance between meditation, study and work. It is designed to create the best possible conditions for a person to make spiritual progress.

A typical day at a Theravada Monastery

4am   - Rise (In Thailand, this might well be 2.30am.)

5am   - Puja (worship) and meditation

7am   - Breakfast and morning meeting

8am   - Work

10.30am - Receiving and eating the main meal of the day (In some places this includes going on an alms round to receive the food from local villagers. Elsewhere, lay Buddhists come to a monastery to prepare and serve a meal to the monks and nuns.)

12.30pm - Tea break

1pm   - Work

5pm   - Tea break, time to rest and talk

7.30pm - Evening Puja and meditation, followed by a talk from a senior member of the community

10 - 11pm- Bed

(This timetabble is based on information about the Theravadin community at Amaravati, in Hertfordshire, given by Denise Cush in Buddhists in Britain Today.*)*

Questions

- Explain in your own words how monks and lay people help and support one another in Theravada Buddhism. What would happen if they did not do so?
- Looking at the timetable above, what would be, for you, the hardest thing about life in a monastery? What would be the most attractive?

Preparing for a spell as a monk...

First your head is shaved. Members of your family may help.

Then you are robed - first in the white robe. This is the colour worn by anagarikas, those who have taken the first step towards the monastic life.

At the end of the ceremony you sit in the shrine room as an ordained monk, paying your respects to the senior monks under whom you will study.

Uposatha days, which fall on the 1st, 8th, 15th and 23rd days of the lunar month (the Full Moon, the New Moon, and the days in between them) are important for bhikkus. They meet together on Uposatha days to recite the Patimokka - the 227 rules in the Vinaya which they try to keep. These days were probably important for people before Buddhism, and were adopted by the Sangha as days for their meetings.

Reciting the Patimokka.

Although the bhikku has no possessions, he carries with him several items which belong to the vihara. The items vary slightly from sect to sect, but they usually include:-

- **An offering bowl.** The word bhikku means 'one who shares'. A bhikku does not beg for food, a lay Buddhist shares food with him. Lay believers give food freely and place it in this bowl. They are grateful for the opportunity to do this, for it reminds them of the Dharma and gains them merit.
- **A razor.** To keep the head and face clean of hair.
- **A water strainer.** To avoid swallowing living things unknowingly. This is really a symbol of the respect a Buddhist has for life and living things.
- **A needle.** To darn the robes. As well as being a practical tool, this is a symbol of poverty.

A bhikku gets up very early in the morning, before sunrise. He washes, dresses, and cleans the area around him. After morning meditation and prayers, he leaves the vihara with his bowl to receive food from lay believers. He returns to the monastery to eat his meal. Remember - he must do this before midday! Having eaten, he learns about the Dhamma from the theras and devotes the rest of the day to study and teaching the Dhamma by discussion.

Activities

Key Elements

1 What is a vihara?
2 What conditions have to be fulfilled before becoming a bhikku?
3 Make a list of the preparations a man has to make before becoming a bhikku.
4 What is the robe a symbol of?
5 What is Patimokkha?
6 List the items a bhikku carries.

Think About It

7 Make a list of 'attachments' you have - possessions which you feel you couldn't live without. Beside each one write how that item could make you unhappy, or suffer. (Your Walkman may break down!)
8 If you could possess only five things, what would they be? Why?
9 Why do you think bhikkus take more precepts than lay believers?

Images of the Buddha

Theravada Buddhism emphasises that the Buddha was an ordinary man. The only difference between him and any other man was that he was enlightened. This belief is clearly reflected in Theravadin images of the Buddha.

For several hundred years there were no images of the Buddha (the only monuments were stupas), but nowadays there are probably millions of statues, pictures and carvings depicting the Buddha. In most of them he is shown in one of just three positions: standing, sitting or lying down.

If the statue depicts the Buddha standing, one hand raised may illustrate protection . When sitting, the position of his hands may indicate meditation, teaching or enlightenment. The Buddha lying down usually indicates his death and entry into Pari-Nibbana. The position of the Buddha's hands shows what the particular image represents (see page 111).

Most Theravadin images of the Buddha depict some or all of his Thirty-Two Characteristics. He is usually shown with very long ear-lobes - a symbol of honour. A round mark on his forehead is known as the Eye of Wisdom, and symbolises the Buddha'a ability to see the reality of life.

This is what a Christian monk wrote on seeing a figure of the dying Buddha:-

I am able to approach the Buddhas barefoot and undisturbed, my feet in wet grass, wet sand. Then the silence of the extraordinary faces. The great smiles. Huge and yet subtle. Filled with every possibility, questioning nothing, knowing everything, rejecting nothing, the peace not of emotional resignation but of Madhyamika [the Middle Way], of sunyata [emptiness], that has seen through every question without trying to discredit anyone or anything...Such peace, such silence, can be frightening. I was knocked over with a rush of relief and thankfulness at the obvious clarity of the figures, the clarity and fluidity of shape and line, the design of the monumental bodies composed into the rock shape and landscape, figure, rock and tree. And the sweep of bare rock sloping away on the other side of the hollow, where you can go back and see different aspects of the figures.

Looking at these figures I was suddenly, almost forcibly, jerked clean out of the habitual, half-tired vision of things, and an inner clearness, clarity, as if exploding from the rocks themselves, became evident and obvious. The...evidence of the reclining figure, the smile, the sad smile of Ananda standing with arms folded [at his head]...The thing about all this is that there is no puzzle, no problem, and really no "mystery". All problems are resolved and everything is clear. The rock, all matter, all life, is charged with dharmakaya [the Buddha Truth]...everything is emptiness and everything is compassion.

The dying Buddha with Ananda at his head.

Another Westerner - a Russian - described his experience on seeing the statue of 'The Buddha With Sapphire Eyes' in what is now Sri Lanka.

> *I began to feel the strange effect which the Buddha's face produced on me. All the gloom that rose from the depths of my soul seemed to clear up. It was as if the Buddha's face communicated its calm to me. Everything that up to now had troubled me and appeared so serious and important, now became so small, insignificant and unworthy of notice, that I only wondered how it could ever have affected me. And I felt that no matter how agitated, troubled, irritated and torn with contradictory thoughts and feelings a man might be when he came here, he would go away calm, quiet, enlightened, understanding...All Buddhism was in this face, in this gaze...*

Activities

Key Elements

1 What do Theravada Buddhists believe about the Buddha?

Think About It

2 Look at one of the two accounts of seeing Buddha images. Pick out words which sum up the experience. Use these words to write a poem about reflecting on a Buddha image.

Buildings

The design of Theravadin Temples varies from country to country, though nearly all contain buildings like those put up after the Buddha's death to house relics of his body. These buildings are known as 'stupas' ('mounds') because they in turn are based on traditional burial mounds.

As a result, stupas are dome-shaped buildings. The dome itself contains the relics. On top of it is usually a pole with discs on it to represent a parasol. This is a symbol of honour as parasols were signs of royalty in ancient India. At the base of the dome are paths so that worshippers may walk around the stupa. This is a symbol that the Buddha should be at the centre of one's life, just as his relics are at the centre of the circumambulation (walking in a circle).

A temple-vihara in Thailand is called a Wat. Nearly every town and village in Thailand has its own wat which is at the heart of the community. Lay people give money to support their local wat, gaining merit for themselves in the process.

The shrine room is the main hall of the wat. As well as containing a shrine with a statue of the Buddha, there are usually other decorations

A simple Theravadin stupa.

around the room, and images telling stories of the Buddha's life. It is here that the bhikkhus worship, and lay believers bring flowers and other gifts to leave at the shrine. The building itself usually faces east, as the Buddha is supposed to have been facing east when he became enlightened.

Inside a Wat there may be many buildings and images. People generally make offerings of candles and incense. Sometimes they bring fruit or flowers. Each person makes his or her own act of worship.

In Sri Lanka temples are usually built with highly stylised domes. Like the Indian stupas, they contain a relic of the Buddha, one of his disciples or an arahat. They are known as Dagobas, which means 'relic chamber'.

The idea of the dagoba crossed the sea to Burma, where the name changed to Pagoda. Once again relics of the Buddha and his followers are kept here. They can be large and very ornate structures, decorated in gold leaf, to which lay believers add more leaves out of respect for the Three Treasures - the Buddha, the Dhamma, and the Sangha - gaining merit at the same time.

Although Theravada Buddhist temples vary in design in different parts of the world, they tend to have common features.
1. A shrine room, for worship.
2. A meditation room, also used for Vinaya rituals.
3. Living quarters for the bhikkhus.
4. A relic mound, properly called dagoba. (A stupa is really the place which contains a dagoba.)
5. A bo-tree is usually planted in the temple grounds to symbolise the Buddha's enlightenment.

A Dagoba in Sri Lanka.

Activities

Key Elements

1 What is a stupa?
2 What shape is it?
3 What is a Thai temple called?
4 Which direction does it face? Why?
5 What is a dagoba?
6 What is a pagoda?

Activity

• Find out about the directions other religious buildings face - some churches and some mosques, for examples.

Festivals

As Theravada Buddhism is practised differently in different countries according to local customs and traditions, each of these countries has different festivals. However, there are some festivals which occur in all Theravadin countries, and although they may be celebrated slightly differently, they still have much in common.

Wesak

In Sri Lanka, the name of the second month of the year, which roughly corresponds with April-May, is Vesakha. The day of the full moon (an Uposatha day) is held as a festival and named after the month: Wesak.

Wesak is the festival which commemorates the birth, enlightenment and death of the Buddha, and is probably the most important of the Theravadin festivals. Light is used as a symbol of all three aspects of the festival: birth, enlightenment and the entry into Nibbana. Light is also used as a symbol of the rarity of discovering the Dhamma in one lifetime. People light lanterns, carry them through the streets and hang them outside houses.

At Wesak, lay believers make a special effort to make donations to the bhikkus. Some take on the extra five precepts reserved for bhikkhus in addition to the five precepts of Pansil. So, just for the duration of the Wesak festival, they will also undertake not to eat after midday, not to sleep in a luxurious bed, not to wear ornamentation or scent, not to go to entertainments, and not to handle money.

Bhikkhus and lay believers will spend the day together in the temple, attending lectures on the scriptures, listening to sermons, chanting and meditating. Outside the temple, there may be processions, and stalls will be set up to give away food and drink to passers by. Wesak is seen as a great opportunity to accumulate merit.

Vassa

The Full Moon in July or August coincides with the beginning of the tropical rainy season in the east. This day is remembered as Asala, commemorating the preaching of the Buddha's first sermon on the Middle Way in the Deer Park at Sarnath, near Benares. This is known as 'Setting in Motion the Wheel of the Law': the Buddha had begun the movement of the Dhamma.

The following day is the beginning of Vassa, a period during which bhikkhus and bhikkunis retreat from their usual life, and spend the rainy season in the vihara studying and meditating.

It is important for everyone to spend some time during the year doing something completely different from their habitual routine, and have a chance to recoup their energy. In tropical countries, the three months of the rainy season are an ideal opportunity to do this. Some laymen and boys become ordained and join the bhikkhus for this period, returning to their homes at the end.

Young boys are dressed as princes, like the young Siddattha, and paraded through the streets in a huge procession to the vihara. There they will give up their expensive clothes, have their heads shaved and enter the vihara. They may stay for one night, for the whole of Vassa, or as the first step towrds full ordination.

The end of the rainy season, in October-November, is marked by another festival called Kathina. The bhikkhus and lay believers have had little contact with each other during Vassa, but now they join up again in celebration. Some families welcome their children home again, others congratulate the bhikkhus on their retreat, for it is believed that they have created merit for the whole community. The bhikkhus are given special food as an offering. This is the time when lay believers contribute robes, bowls, razors and other essential equipment to the vihara.

New Year

Washing a Buddha image at New Year

New Year is an important time for Buddhists. It is a symbol of new life, a time to make a new start and to generate positive karma. And just as one year melts into the next, so rebirth follows rebirth.

New Year in Burma and Thailand falls at the beginning of Spring, in April. The day starts by taking gifts to the local temple in the form of presents for the bhikkhus and offerings to the Buddha.

Afterwards, lay believers set fish free in the neighbourhood rivers. April can be very hot in Burma and Thailand, so hot that small rivers dry up leaving fish stranded and on the verge of death. In the days leading up to New Year, lay Buddhists collect the fish and set them free in the large rivers at New Year. By doing this, they not only gain merit, but also symbolise the respect that Buddhists have for all life.

As a symbol of newness and a fresh start, images of the Buddha are washed in cool, scented water. Some people, particularly the children, don't stop there: they start to splash the water over each other, and the afternoon is spent in water fights. Children lie in wait for each other, or chase each other through the streets, to throw water. Everyone gets soaked.

The festival lasts for three days altogether. The second and third days are spent in celebration, playing games, flying kites, dancing and performing traditional plays. The end of the third day is marked by worship at the temple. Once again, lay believers make offerings and recite Pansil. Beginning another year reminds Buddhists how fortunate they are to have been born as human beings who have found the Dhamma.

Celebrating the New Year is not a solemn occasion! Be prepared to get soaking wet.

Activities

Key Elements

1 What does Wesak commemorate?
2 What does Asala commemorate?
3 What is the rainy season called?
4 What is the festival at the end of the rainy season called?
5 Why are fish set free at New Year?

Think About It

6 At Wesak, people often wear white. Why do you think this is?
7 Why do you think lay believers take on the extra five precepts at Wesak?
8 Do you think it is important to have a break during the year? What activities do you do during the holidays to recoup your energy?
9 Do you make New Year's resolutions? What sort of resolutions do you make? Do you keep them? Why do we make resolutions at New Year?

Assignments

1 Theravada Buddhism has a strong history in Cambodia. Find out about Cambodia's recent history, and why the practice of Buddhism has declined there.
2 Of all the theories of what happens at death, rebirth is the most widely believed. Conduct a survey in your school on beliefs about death. Which beliefs are most common? Present the results of your survey in the form of a report.
3 Design a Wat which would fit in well in your area. Justify the decisions you make in your design. Remember, Buddhism adapts well to local cirumstances.
4 Design decorations for the walls of a shrine room based on some of the stories about the Buddha's life that you know. Justify your use of symbols.
5 Find out more about the symbols used to represent the characteristics of the Buddha.

8

Mahayana Buddhism

Distinctive Ideas

The word 'Mahayana' means 'great vehicle'. It was invented by Mahayanists to contrast their beliefs with those of other Buddhist sects, especially the Theravada. It was used to mock the Theravadins by calling their beliefs 'Hinayana', or 'small vehicle'.

It isn't that the Mahayanists disagree with the Theravadins. All Buddhism is based on the same principles, outlined in chapter two. But Mahayana Buddhism builds on those principles to create a different outlook. Mahayanists therefore claim that their 'vehicle' is 'great' because their beliefs are more comprehensive and enable more people to benefit from them.

The main difference is this:

- **Mahayanists believe that all beings have the capacity to become Buddhas and, eventually, all will.**
- **Theravadins teach that some disciples of the Buddha may become enlightened, but they will never be as great as Siddhattha himself.**

The Mahayanists agree that the Buddha was an enlightened human being in history, but claim that the important thing about him was his enlightenment. Therefore the details of the history of the Buddha are unimportant to the Mahayanist; in fact, it does not even matter if he never existed at all. What matters is that all beings possess Buddhahood, in the same way as they all possess happiness or sadness or anger. And all beings are capable of revealing Buddhahood, regardless of their social background; regardless even of which religion they practise.

All this is made clear in the Lotus Sutra:-

"All beings of this world believe that Shakyamuni Buddha left the Palace of the Shakyas, sat under a linden tree near the Castle Gaya and attained enlightenment. However, my disciples, you must understand this: it is actually an almost infinite and immeasurable time since I attained Buddhahood."

We can calculate the amount of time since the Buddha claims to have become enlightened according to the Lotus Sutra. We need to know some facts first.

1. This is a number in classical Chinese: "Go hyaku sen man noku nayuta asogi." Go=5; Hyaku=100; Sen=1,000; Man=10,000; (N)oku=100,000; Nayuta=10 to the power of 4; Asogi=10 to the power of 51. First of all we need to multiply these numbers together.

2. According to ancient oriental astronomy, "sekai" is a 'world system' equivalent to our solar system. Ten million sekai form a "sho-sen sekai", or "minor world system". A thousand sho-sen sekai form a "chu-sen sekai", or "medium world system"; and a thousand "chu-sen sekai"

form a "dai-sen sekai", or "major world system".

3. An aeon is a unit of time.

Now, the Lotus Sutra says:-

"Suppose someone crushes go hyaku sen man noku nayuta asogi major world systems into particles of dust. He then travels east dropping one particle of dust every time he has passed go hyaku sen man noku nayuta asogi world systems. He continues doing this until he has finished dropping all the particles.

"Now, suppose all the world systems he has passed, whether they have received a particle of dust or not, are themselves crushed into particles of dust. Let one particle of dust represent one aeon. The number of aeons which has passed since I attained Buddhahood is that number multiplied by go hyaku sen man noku nayuta asogi."

All we need to know now is how long an aeon is. Well, suppose there is a mountain eighteen kilometres high. Once every hundred years a crane flies across the top of the mountain and brushes the peak softly with one of its wings. An aeon is the amount of time it takes for the crane to wear the mountain down to nothing.

Good luck with the calculation!

All this means that the Buddha is eternal and unlimited. In fact, he can, and does, appear at many different points in history in all the different parts of the universe to teach the Dharma. And when he teaches the Dharma, he does so in a way which is suited to the needs and capacities of the people. The Buddha is therefore said to be skilful-in-means (upaya-kaushalya), because the means he uses to teach the dharma are skilfully thought out.

Refer back to the story of the Wise Doctor from the Lotus Sutra (see page 62). Here the Doctor (Buddha) has to use upaya, a skilful device, to save his sons (all beings). The skilful device is actually a lie - he says he is dead - but it is necessary to achieve the far greater goal of saving his sons' lives.

The story of the Wise Doctor begins:-

'Disciples, it is a rare event to see the Buddha. If people realize how rare it is, they will yearn after him and find the root of enlightenment in their hearts. It is for this reason that the Buddha prophesies his own death, although he does not die in reality.'

And the story ends:-

'Now, my disciples, do you call this wise doctor a liar?'

'No, my Lord,' they answer.

Then the Buddha says,

'It is the same for me. I attained enlightenment an almost infinite and immeasurable time ago. But now, like the Doctor, I predict my death. Let no one accuse me of deceit!'

He is making the point that, although his body may pass away, the Buddha nature will never die. Even birth and death are skilful means to enable the Buddha to teach the Dharma to all beings.

But why should the Buddha want to use so many skilful means? The answer given by Mahayana Buddhism is that, out of compassion, (karuna), the Buddha always wants to respond to people's needs, and to relieve suffering. He is able to do this because of his wisdom (prajna) to see everything as it is. So the Buddha's skill-in-means (upaya) is a combination of wisdom (prajna) and compassion (karuna).

Activities

Key Elements

1 What is 'great' about Mahayana?
2 How does the Mahayana view of the Buddha differ from the Theravadin?
3 Why does it not matter to the Mahayanist whether or not the Buddha Shakyamuni existed?
4 What is upaya?
5 Complete this equation: Pr.... + Ka.... = Up.....

Think About It

6 How would a Mahayanist answer the charge that Shakyamuni did not say the words attributed to him in the Mahayana scriptures?

Activity

• Write the rules of football (or cricket!) for a) a four-year-old boy, b) a four-year-old girl, c) someone your own age, d) a rugby player. Use upaya!

Buddhism in the Far East

Buddhism adapts itself to accommodate local beliefs and traditions, and this is especially true of Mahayana Buddhism. Mahayana Buddhism aims to appeal to every kind of person, emphasising that everyone has the ability to reveal Buddhahood. This flexibility is particularly evident in the way Buddhism was accepted in China.

The Mahayana Schools insisted that the teachings of the Buddha reveal the truth about the nature of life, but that those teachings should be presented in different ways to different people. When Buddhism arrived in China it encountered Conficianism and Taoism, which were the greatest influences on Chinese thought. They were systems of thought which promoted practicality, tolerance, duty and organisation, and they influenced the way in which Buddhism presented itself.

It is not known exactly when Buddhism was introduced to China; however, it certainly existed there in the first century CE. The first task to be undertaken was the translation of the Mahayana scriptures from Sanskrit to Chinese, and the Chinese scholars were masterful at it. Their translations are so accurate that it is possible to translate back from Chinese and achieve a text almost identical to the original.

The character of Chinese Buddhism was set in the 6th century CE by an Indian Buddhist called Bodhidharma who settled in China. He summarised Buddhism as he understood it:-

1. The teachings of the Buddha have been passed on by word of mouth exactly as they were taught.
2. The scriptures are not depended upon as sources of the Buddha's teachings.
3. Buddhism points directly to the inner nature of human beings.
4. Since it sees into one's inner nature, Buddhahood can be revealed from within.

Bodhidharma claimed that this summary was an accurate reflection of the spirit of the Buddha's teaching, and based the practice of his form of Buddhism on meditation, dhyana in Sanskrit. Dhyana was translated into Chinese as Ch'an, and later into Japanese as Zen.

Images of Bodhidharma generally show him looking fierce and determined.

From China, Buddhism moved to Korea which it reached in the latter half of the fourth century CE. The form of Buddhism that reached Korea was entirely Chinese Mahayana. Once again it was adapted to accommodate local conditions. The type of Buddhism that passed through Korea was largely Zen mixed with that of the Chinese Buddhist thinker, T'ien T'ai. T'ien T'ai's work involved classifying all of the Buddhist teachings.

From Korea, Buddhism was introduced to Japan in the middle of the sixth century CE, and once again it took on a new, distinctive character adapted to the Japanese culture. Buddhism was formally accepted by the Regent of Japan, Shotoku Taishi (593-622CE), and it was the Japanese tradition that once the ruler accepted a religion, it was to be practised by his subjects, too. Shotoku himself contributed greatly to the spread of Buddhism in Japan. He built monasteries, shrines and temples; he encouraged artists and craftsmen to depict Buddhist ideas in their art; and he himself wrote commentaries on many important Mahayana texts including the The Lotus Sutra, which T'ien T'ai of China thought to be the highest of all Buddhist scriptures.

At least ten Mahayana sects came to Japan from China, via Korea, and all were adapted to the Japanese culture. Some developed further to form new sects, the most important of which is probably that founded by the 13th century bhikku, Nichiren, based on T'ien T'ai's Buddhism.

However, even though under Shotoku Buddhism became the state religion, there was still great rivalry between the sects, and the distinction between bhikku and lay believer became blurred. Some politicians became bhikkus, and some bhikkus became politicians. Monasteries owned vast amounts of land and employed thousands of people, and so the Sangha included both monastic and lay Buddhists.

Although the progressive Mahayanists broke away from the more conservative Theravadins, they do not consider themselves to be a separate school. Rather they consider that they have extended the central teachings of Theravada so as to be appropriate for all human beings. Today there is only one sect in the Theravada School, but there are still many Mahayana sects around the world.

Activities

Key Elements

1 Which countries in the main practise Mahayana Buddhism?
2 Which sect of Buddhism did Bodhidharma found?
3 Why is T'ien T'ai important to Mahayana Buddhists?

Think About It

4 What do you think the name Bodhidharma means? Why do you think Bodhidharma chose this name for himself?
5 Put Bodhidharma's four principles into your own words.

Buildings

Mahayana temples in a modern country like Japan may take the form of a concrete hall on a busy city street. However, traditional Mahayana places of worship derive from the Theravada stupa. In Burma, the stupa developed into a taller building called a pagoda. In China and Japan, the pagoda has its own distictive style. It generally consists of a number of square storeys, each with its own sloped and gently-curved roof, stacked one on top the other. Like stupas, pagodas house relics or precious antiquities.

Traditional Mahayana temples are actually complexes of many buildings. Central to the temple campus is the shrine-room where large images are housed. The images will vary from temple to temple, but often there will be a group of three Great Buddhas, or a Buddha and two Bodhisattvas, perhaps with images of sixteen or eighteen chief disciples.

The temple complex in the Summer Palace, Beijing.

Also in the complex will be accommodation for monks and nuns; in Japan accommodation will be provided for married priests and their families. Pagodas function as reliquaries (places to house relics), though many are designed so they cannot be entered. If they can be entered, entry is often restricted to a few chief priests. Temples may also have a meeting hall, a meditation hall, a library, administrative buildings, and gardens.

Question
• What would you find inside a pagoda?

Worship

As in the Theravada tradition, Mahayana worship tends not to be congregational, although there are usually opportunities to get together in shared activities.

Bowing is a very important symbolic gesture in most Buddhist cultures. In Japan, for example, children bow to their teachers and even their parents; adults bow to monks and nuns; the young bow to the old; workers bow to their bosses. Bowing is an acknowedgement of someone having more experience of life, or perhaps a deeper understanding of spiritual matters. It is therefore a symbol of respect. And the lower the bow, the greater is the respect being shown. It is natural, then, for Buddhists to bow deeply before objects of worship.

Usually bowing is performed from a kneeling position. Hands are held together at the head, lips and chest symbolizing respect in thought, word and action. Sometimes the worshipper will push himself forward until he is lying full-length on the ground before the shrine.

Offerings are made at the shrine as a mark of respect for the Buddha nature. It is common for seven kinds of offerings to be made at a shrine. Two bowls of water, essential for drinking and washing, symbolize hospitality, while flowers, incense, lamps, perfume and food represent the five senses. These seven offerings are placed in seven different bowls. Occasionally all seven bowls will contain water, symbolic of the seven offerings.

In all forms of Buddhism, chanting accompanies ceremonial acts. The chanting in itself is a soothing act which leads to greater self-confidence and a pure mind. Chanting often expresses lovingkindness to all beings and so can calm down an aggressive person. It is also believed to activate the Great Buddhas and Bodhisattvas - the protective forces of the universe - to work in favour of the chanter.

A Tibetan monk throws himself full-length on the ground as a sign of devotion and personal dedication. The practice is called prostration.

Activities

Key Elements

1 Why are hands held together at the head, lips and chest during Mahayana worship?
2 List the offerings made at a Mahayana shrine. What do they symbolize?
3 Why do Buddhists chant?

Think About It

4 Why do you think it is not important for Buddhists to worship together?
5 Apart from bowing, list other ways in which we use our bodies to show respect.
6 When choosing a gift, what factors do people take into account to ensure that the gift is appropriate?
7 What would you give to a) a mother at home with a new baby, b) a friend in hospital recovering from an operation, c) a new next-door neighbour, d) someone who has died?
8 Why do people put flowers on graves?
9 Why do crowds at football matches chant together? How do you think it makes them feel?

Bodhisattvas

The Mahayana image of the ideal unenlightened human being is one who acts entirely out of compassion, without thinking about him- or herself. Such a person is called a Bodhisattva. The word 'Bodhisattva' means 'Enlightenment Being' - in other words, someone who wishes to become enlightened. A Bodhisattva is one who, in order to become enlightened, actually delays enlightenment itself in order to help others to enlightenment. In this way, the Bodhisattva can become enlightened more quickly.

Read the last two sentences again. This is an example of a paradox. Enlightenment comes more quickly by delaying it! And we have also seen that Mahayanists believe that all beings are already Buddhas in any case!

This paradox can be solved by thinking of a journey to see someone you love. Sometimes the shortest route is not the quickest. In the same way, choosing the Bodhisattva path actually helps shorten the journey to Buddhahood. And in reality, everything you love about the person at the end of your journey exists inside you already. The journey simply gets you nearer the physical body of that person. Similarly, Buddhahood exists within all the time, and speaking of 'attaining' or 'reaching' Buddhahood is just a traditional way of presenting the Bodhisattva path.

There are four stages on the Bodhisattva path:-

1. Intention. The Bodhisattva must be sincere in his or her search for enlightenment. The Mahayana sutras tell many stories to illustrate this point. For example, in the Samyuktagama Sutra is a story of a small boy who sees the Buddha pass by. He earnestly wants to make an offering, but has nothing to give. He therefore makes a mud pie which he dedicates to the Buddha. As a result, he was later reborn as King Asoka, the great Buddhist emperor who ruled over much of India.

Intention and sincerity are important on the path because they give the Bodhisattva determination to reach enlightenment. The following myth shows how difficult the Bodhisattva path can be:-

Once upon a time there was an earnest seeker of the true path named Sadaprarudita. He cast aside every temptation for profit or honour and sought the path at the risk of his life. One day a voice from heaven came to him saying, 'Sadaprarudita! Go straight towards the east. Do not think of either heat or cold; pay no attention to worldly praise or scorn, do not be bothered by discriminations of good or evil, but just keep going east. In the far east you will find a true teacher and will gain Enlightenment.'

Sadaprarudita was very pleased to get this definite instruction and immediately started on his journey eastward. Sometimes he slept where night found him in a lonely field or in the wild mountains.

Being a stranger in foreign lands, he suffered many humiliations; once he sold himself into slavery, selling his own flesh out of hunger, but at last he found the true teacher and asked for his instruction. There is a saying, 'Good things are costly,' and Sadaprarudita found it true in his case, for he had many difficulties on his journey in search of the path. He had no money to buy some flowers and incense to offer the teacher. He tried to sell his services but could find no one to hire him. There seemed to be an evil spirit hindering him every way he turned. The path to Enlightenment is a hard one and it may cost a man his life.

At last Sadaprarudita reached the presence of the teacher himself and then he had a new difficulty. He had no paper on which to take notes and no brush or ink to write with. Then he pricked his wrist with a dagger and took notes in his own blood. In this way he secured the precious truth.

Some versions of this story relate that Sadaprarudita tore off his skin to write on and used his bone as a pen!

2. Vow. We have seen that the Bodhisattva must be thoroughly determined to become enlightened. The second stage on the path is known as pranidhana in Sanskrit. It is usually translated as 'vow', but really means 'fixation'.

The idea is that whatever the mind fixes itself on becomes real. If you are determined to do something, you will!

The Bodhisattva makes two vows: first, to become a Buddha; second, to lead all beings to enlightenment.

3. The Course of the Bodhisattva (Bodhisattva-charya). At this stage, having developed the intention and taken the vow, the Bodhisattva is able to set out along the path itself.

The path consists of developing the Six Perfections (paramitas). We looked at these on page 70, since they form the basis for the morality and lifestyle of Mahayana Buddhists. The perfections are:

a) **Charity (dana):** the perfection of giving. The generosity of giving without expecting anything in return.

b) **Morality (sila):** the perfection of goodness. Thoughts, words and acts which are pure because they are based on deep respect for all life.

c) **Patience (kshanti):** the perfection of composure. The confidence to accept people and things as they are.

d) **Vigour (virya):** the perfection of energy. A natural, persistent effort to work for the benefit of all beings.

e) **Meditation (dhyana):** the perfection of concentration. A constant clarity of mind and perception to see all situations as they really are.

f) **Wisdom (prajna):** the perfection of wise understanding. Insight into the true nature of all dharmas; the realization that everything is empty (sunya).

The Avatamsaka Sutra states:

'Charity and Morality make the foundation on which to build a great castle. Patience and Vigour are the walls of the castle that protect it aginst enemies from outside. Meditation and Wisdom are the personal armour that protects one against the assaults of life and death.'

4. Buddhahood. In this final stage, the Bodhisattva becomes enlightened. Having undertaken the path, the Bodhisattva realizes that the actions he or she has made in the service of other people are the actions of a Buddha. In other words, the Bodhisattva is a Buddha all along. Taking the path is the way to understand this.

Activity

• Read the last three sentences again. Then explain them in your own words.

Activities

Key Elements

1 What does 'Bodhisattva' mean?
2 Why does a Bodhisattva delay his or her enlightenment?
3 Outline the four stages on the Bodhisattva path.
4 What are the six paramitas?

Think About It

5 Find out what 'altruism' means. Is there such a thing as a completely altruistic act? If you help an old person across the road, do you get anything out of it? What about feeling good? Would feeling good motivate you to do it again?
6 Look back through this book. Write a list of paradoxes you come across.
7 Is intention more important than action? Think about killing, for example.
8 Write about a time when someone (you?) had good intentions which, when put into action, went wrong. What was the outcome?
9 If you really want to achieve something, do obstacles stop you? Or do they make you try harder? Why?

Mahayana Images

As the Mahayana movement grew, so did the mythology of Buddhism. Great Bodhisattvas came to be seen as supernatural figures symbolizing spiritual qualities. They became focuses of worship as beings who could save people - even whole countries.

Images of Great Bodhisattvas and Buddhas in the Mahayana tradition function as more than reminders of their spiritual qualities. Mahayana believers see images as possessing the spirit and power of the being they represent. They therefore hold a position of honour in Mahayana worship. Sometimes scriptures or relics are placed inside them; sometimes they are even given internal organs modelled out of clay.

Avalokitesvara

The most popular of the Great Bodhisattvas is Avalokitesvara. He is a symbol of the compassion of the Bodhisattva. In fact his Sanskrit name means 'The Lord Who Looks Down (with compassion)', while in China 'he' is female and is called Kuan-shih-yin, which means 'The One Who Takes Notice Of The Cries Of The World.' The Japanese name, Kannon, comes from this. So widely known and respected is Kannon that the Canon electrical and photographic company is named after him/her. Buddhists in all Mahayana countries, worship and pray to Avalokitesvara for help in their daily lives.

There are many stories about Avalokitesvara. In the Amitayurdhyana Sutra, he and another Bodhisattva appear as the Buddha's attendants. In the Lotus Sutra it says that he takes on thirty-three different forms to save the people. He even appears in the worlds of ghosts or animals. In Chinese art he sometimes appears as a bull, warning a butcher away from his murderous livelihood. It is Tibetan custom to think of the Dalai Lama as an incarnation of Avalokitesvara, or Chenrezig as he is known there.

In pictures, Avalokitesvara is shown crowned like a prince and dressed in royal garments. This symbolizes his position as a Great Being on the one hand, and his mission to help all beings on the other. He holds a lotus bud in his left hand, as a symbol of the ability of all beings to 'bloom' into Buddhahood. Sometimes his hands are cupped together, like a lotus bud, as a symbol of his willingness to grant wishes to those who call upon him.

Manjusri

An image of Kwan-shih-yin in a Chinese Buddhist shrine.

An image of Manjushri - notice the sword of wisdom with which he cuts through ignorance.

Another important Bodhisattva is Manjusri, which means 'Sweet Glory'. If Avalokitesvara represents compassion, then Manjusri represents the Buddha's wisdom. His special task is to destroy ignorance about the world, and awaken spiritual knowledge (prajna).

He is therefore depicted as holding a lotus supporting a copy of the Prajna-paramita Sutras. In his other hand he is wielding a flaming sword, a symbol of wisdom cutting away ignorance. He is said to protect teachers of the Dharma.

Maitreya

One of the earliest Bodhisattvas referred to in the Mahayana tradition is Maitreya, 'The Kindly One', who is even mentioned in Theravada writings. Mahayanists say that Maitreya is, or will be, the next major incarnation of the Buddha to come to earth. In China he is known as Mi-lo-fo, and is often represented as a large, jolly, pot-bellied man carrying a sack of presents for children. The sack is called pu-tai, and Mi-lo-fo is often named after this sack. In the West he is better known as the 'Laughing Buddha'.

Mi-lo-fo - otherwise known as 'the laughing Buddha'

Amitabha

Finally we must look at a Bodhisattva who went on to become a Buddha, traditions about whom have become of central importance to the Pure Land Schools of the Far East.

The larger Sukhavati-vyuha Sutra tells of a king called Dharmakara who heard a sermon of the Buddha. He was so impressed that he left his kingdom and decided that he would become a Buddha. He had heard that Buddhas preside over pure lands, and he determined that when he became a Buddha, his Pure Land would have the best qualities of all of them. Altogether he made forty-six Bodhisattva vows, the eighteenth of which reads, "If, after my obtaining Buddhahood, all beings should not sincerely desire to be born into my Pure Land, and if they should not be born by reciting my name ten times (except those who have slandered the Dharma), may I not attain the highest Enlightenment." Dharmakara attained enlightenment, and as a Buddha is known as Amitabha which means 'Infinite Light'. In China he is called Amita, and in Japan, Amida.

In the Pure Land (Sukhavati), beings have eternal life, unless they wish to return to earth as Bodhisattvas to help the living:-

In this Pure Land there are infinite Light and everlasting Life. Those who reach this haven will never return to that world of delusion.

Indeed, this Pure Land, where the flowers perfume the air with wisdom and the birds sing the holy Dharma, is the final destination for all mankind.

In order to be reborn in the Pure Land, you have to fulfil certain conditions. You have to really want it; you must have faith in Amitabha; you must gain merit and dedicate it towards rebirth. In addition you must recite the Buddha's name in the form "Namo Amitabhaya Buddhaya" (Sk), or "Namu Amida Butsu" (Jap). This recitation is called Nembutusu. Amitabha therefore represents the Buddha nature. By reciting the mantra, it is believed you can draw out your own Buddha nature and achieve happiness.

A belief in rebirth in the Pure Land has provided hope to many people when their lives have been hard. The Pure Land school of Buddhism (Shin) has therefore had great influence in Japan, especially in the years following the Second World War.

Trikaya

About 300CE Mahayana ideas on the nature of Buddhas were summarized in a system called Trikaya, or the Three Bodies. According to this theory, Buddhahood has three aspects:-

1. Nirmana-kaya, or Tranformation Body. The Transformation Body refers to the physical body which the Buddha uses to teach the Dharma to human beings. At death, the physical body falls away, and the Buddha himself melts into the Buddha nature of the universe. Some Mahayana Buddhists see great leaders of other religions and even political movements as Transformation Bodies of the Buddha.
2. Sambhoga-kaya, or Enjoyment Body
   The Enjoyment Body is that which is seen in visions or meditation. While it is not a physical body, it is in no way less 'real' than the Transformation Body, for it teaches directly to people regardless of time or geographical location. Each Enjoyment Body Buddha presides over a Pure Land. Amitabha may be seen as an Enjoyment Body.
3. Dharma-kaya, or Truth Body.

The Dharma Body is the collection of qualities which go to make up the Buddha nature: knowledge, wisdom, compassion, determination, energy, and so on. It includes the very nature of reality: emptiness. Thus it is the real nature or Body of the Buddha.

The point about Trikaya is that Buddhahood is very difficult to understand. This is an attempt to make it easier to grasp by looking at it in these three different ways.

Think of the Buddha nature as H_2O. What is H_2O? We might at first say that it is water. Well, yes, it is water; but is that all it is? No; it is also steam; it is also ice. And each of these can take different forms: snow, fog, hail, and so on. Each of these forms, or 'Bodies', is very different in appearance and structure from the others, and yet all are H_2O. Similarly, each of the Trikaya represents a different form of the same Buddha nature.

Question
• How might Trikaya help a Buddhist understand the Buddha nature?

The Sangha

In India, it seemed quite natural for a person to decide to leave home and family in order to follow a spiritual quest and, in doing so, Siddhartha had been following a long-established tradition. However, Mahayana Buddhism spread to countries, like China, where family members felt a great responsibility for each other, and it seemed wrong to leave them to become a bhikshu (the Sanskrit Mahayana word for Bhikku). In time, however, when Buddhism had shown that it could be adapted to its local circumstances, the Monastic Sangha became accepted.

In the Mahayana Buddhism of China and Japan, the Three Jewels are regarded as a system of precepts. In order to reveal Buddhahood, Mahayana Buddhists have faith and trust in the religious significance of the Buddha, the truth of the Dharma, and the social and moral importance of the Sangha. It is important to develop the qualities of wisdom and compassion.

In Japan there has always been a close relationship between the Sangha and the lay government. In some cases, bhikshus acted as advisers to the government. Today the Japanese bhikshu acts as a source of guidance for lay believers. In some respects he resembles an English parish priest. (In fact, he is often called a 'priest'.) He may be in charge of his own temple which is supported by the local people for whom he is responsible.

In the nineteenth century a law was passed allowing Japanese bhikshus to marry, and many do. In some cases, 'priesthood' has become a family tradition, and the administration of a particular temple may be passed from father to son. Instead of the Theravadin yellow cotton robe, the Japanese bhikshu may wear a grey or black silk one, often with a small tear sewn up as a symbol of poverty.

The Mahayana bhikshu does not travel to teach the Dharma. In many sects it is the lay Sangha that spreads the Dharma to the people. If the bhikshu has his own 'parish' temple, he will conduct ceremonies and teach the Dharma there. Otherwise he attends 'services' in his monastery which few lay people attend.

Even though the Mahayana bhikshu leads a more worldly life than the Theravadin bhikku, much of his lifestyle is traditional. Individually, he is poor and owns few possessions. Bhikshus are usually vegetarian, living off the food grown around the temple. The bhikshus of some sects receive alms from lay believers in the area, but most work in the temple gardens to produce their own food. In addition they perform the domestic chores that have to be done: cooking, cleaning and laundry.

For the Mahayanist, since the Dharma incorporates all life, all work done with sincere effort is done for the Three Jewels.

Activities

- Draw Manjusri, and label the symbols.
- Draw a cartoon strip of the story of Amida Buddha.

Activities

Key Elements

1 Why are images of Bodhisattvas and Buddhas important in Mahayana worship?
2 What does Avalokitesvara mean?
3 What is Avalokitesvara called in China and Japan?
4 What does Manjusri mean?
5 What characteristics of the Buddha do Avalokitesvara and Manjusri symbolize?

6 What does Maitreya mean?
7 Why was it difficult to establish monasteries in China?
8 How do some Mahayana bhikshus symbolise poverty?
9 Describe the roles of, and the relationship between, the monastic and lay Sangha in Mahayana Buddhism.

Think About It

10 When asked where the Pure Land is, a Shin follower patted her heart. What do you think she meant?
11 Find out about Hiroshima and Nagasaki. What hardships would ordinary Japanese citizens have had to endure at the end of the Second World War? How would faith in Nembutsu give hope in times like this?
12 Find out what 'priest' means.
13 Why is it wrong to call a bhikshu a priest?
14 What does it mean to 'work for the Three Jewels'?

Festivals

Mahayana Buddhists remember those who have died on the anniversary of the person's death, during twice-yearly memorial services called Higan and during the observance for honouring the 'spirits' of dead relatives called O-bon. These are not times for sorrow, but festivals to celebrate life.

O-bon

It was a traditional Japanese Mahayana belief that people who had led mean and stingy lives would suffer as 'hungry spirits' for the equivalent of five hundred lifetimes. According to the Shoboenjo Sutra (the Sutra of Meditation on the True Law), there are thirty-six kinds of hungry spirits. Caldron-shaped hungry spirits have no eyes or mouth, because when on earth they attacked and robbed people under cover of night. Vomit-eating hungry spirits feed on the food that people throw up (for five hundred lifetimes!!) because they used to steal food. Hungry spirits without property have had neither food nor drink since birth.

In the Urabon Sutra, Maudgalyayana, one of the Buddha's disciples, tried to save his dead mother, who was a hungry spirit, but was unable to do so. He sought the advice of the Buddha who suggested he offer food to the monks for her sake on the last day of the rainy season retreat. Maudgalyayana did this, and his mother was relieved of her agony. This story is the origin of the O-bon festival.

O-bon is held between the 13th and 15th July each year. Candles, lamps and bonfires are lit to welcome the spirits of the deceased. People play games and go to fairs and dances. They take holidays from work to return to their families, and together they visit the resting places of their deceased relations, although there are no graves in Japan, for land is at a premium and everyone is cremated.

Buddhist priests are invited to homes to recite passages from the sutras and say prayers for the dead. They also carve toba, flat wooden sticks, with prayers and offer these at the family shrine along with fruit and flowers.

Higan

Higan are festivals which mark the spring and autumn equinoxes. They are times of change: seasons begin, days get longer or shorter, the weather changes. They are also times to reflect on life and the many changes which occur, and to pray to change one's life and move towards enlightenment. Higan means 'the other shore', so Japanese Buddhists think about those who have died and pray for their speedy rebirths into fortunate circumstances.

New Year

New Year's Day is another opportunity for Japanese Buddhists to reflect on their lives and make determinations about the future. According to the lunar calendar, spring begins in January, and so Japanese New Year celebrations use symbols of new life, and rice cakes called mushimochi are eaten.

Activities

Key Elements

1 When is O-bon held?
2 What is the purpose of O-bon?
3 What is a toba?
4 When are Higan held?
5 What does Higan mean?
6 Why is New Year important to Buddhists?

Think About It

7 Do you think funerals should be sad or joyous occasions? Why?
8 From what you know about Buddhism, why should Maudgalyayana's offerings enable his mother to be freed from the world of hunger?
9 Make a list of the changes you would like to make in your life. Think also about your character: what characteristics would you like to change? How could you go about it?

Zen

Zen is Buddhism taken to its logical conclusion - or rather its illogical conclusion. Since the path to enlightenment is blocked by attachment to things (tanha), and since in any case everything is sunyata (emptiness), Zen sees it as useless to rely on vows, scripture, rituals or any method to reveal enlightenment.

There are certain devices or methods which we rely on to give order to the world we live in. We rely on our five senses to give us information about the world, and we rely on our brains to process that information. But we know that the information we get is often wrong: we see things that aren't there, we hear noises which don't exist, and our brains sometimes misinterpret the information we get from our senses. We cannot be sure of anything. In any case, as we have seen (especially in chapter five on Sunyata), everything is empty anyway, an illusion. All of the things we usually rely on must be abandoned in order to reveal enlightenment - even logic must go.

Zen was brought to China (where it is called Ch'an) in 520CE by Bodhidharma. A story is told of a disciple who came to him, saying,

"My mind is not at peace; how may it be pacified?"

"Bring it to me and I will pacify it," replied Bodhidharma.

"There," said Bodhidharma, "I have pacified it!"

In other words, all we know of our minds is what they do: they can be restless, preoccupied, calm, anxious. We know nothing of what our minds are. Bodhidharma is pointing out to his disciple that what we have to do to become enlightened is leave our minds behind, because then we will also leave behind all the things the mind does. Then we can concentrate on our enlightenment.

Our basic nature is enlightenment. The problem is that we pile so much on top of it - our worries, our lifestyles, our opinions, our ways of looking at the world, even logic itself - that enlightenment becomes obscured and difficult to find. The only way we can reveal our enlightened nature is to get rid of all the things we put in the way. We have to abandon our traditional ways of thinking.

So, Zen abandons traditional logic and thinking, and tries to get straight to enlightenment. When enlightenment comes, it comes in a flash, like remembering a forgotten name. The Zen word for this flash of enlightenment is satori. It requires action to achieve satori. A Zen pupil was asked by his master why he sat in meditation all day. "To become a Buddha," was the reply. The master picked up a brick and began to rub it. Asked what he was doing, he replied that he was making a mirror. "But no amount of polishing will make the brick a mirror," said the pupil. "And no amount of sitting cross-legged will make you a Buddha," came the retort.

The forms of action to free the mind of traditional patterns of thinking used in Zen are the mondo and the koan. Mondo is a form of rapid question and answer which aims at speeding up thought processes until they are passed over, in the same way as an aeroplane on a runway gets faster and faster by the movement of its wheels on the tarmac until it leaves the ground altogether. A koan is a word or phrase (often a shortened form of a mondo) which cannot be answered by the ordinary mind. It is a riddle and a joke; it smashes conventional thinking. A breakthrough of satori is required to solve it.

Here are some examples:-

Question: What is the Buddha?
Answer: Three pounds of flax.

Question: Is there a teaching no one has taught?
Answer: There is.
Question: What is the teaching no one has taught?
Answer: It is not the mind and it is not the Buddha and it is not a thing.

A temple banner flapped in the wind; two monks were arguing about it. Said one: "The banner moves." Said the other: "The wind moves." They could not agree. The master said, "It is not the wind moving and it is not the banner moving. It is your minds moving."

The master said: "If you have a walking stick, I will give you one; and if you do not have a walking stick, I will take it away from you."

Question: If I have nothing, what should I do?
Answer: Throw it away.

Question: What is the pure Dharmakaya?
Answer: The hedge around the outside loo.

Stop the sound of that bell in the distance.

A girl is crossing the street. Is she the younger or the older sister?

It is pouring now; how would you stop it?

What is your original face before you were born?

How do you react to these examples? With frustration? With anger? That is because you are looking at them as sensible questions or statements. But they are not! They are designed to shock you - all of Zen is. They are nonsense - that is non-sense. They make no sense. Nor does Zen. They take you away from the world of logical sense into the world of satori. And how can you describe satori? You can't: not using logical descriptions, anyway.

One Zen master said, "There's nothing much to this Buddhism. Now that I am enlightened, I'm just as miserable as I was before."

Activities

Key Elements

1 What does Zen mean?
2 Why does Zen not rely on methods to reveal satori?
3 Who brought Zen (Ch'an) to China?
4 What is mondo?
5 What is a koan?
6 How can you stand in the rain without getting wet? (What??)

Think About It

7 Think of times when your senses have deceived you.
8 How do you know when you are dreaming. How do you know you are not dreaming now?
9 Does Zen make sense to you? If so, why??
10 Is this a question?

Assignments

1. Write a diary entry of a Nembutsu (Shin) survivor of the nuclear attack on Hiroshima.
2. Look again at the buildings that go to form a Mahayana temple. Design a temple complex.
3. Compose a drama using symbolic acts only - no words. Remember, this is not a mime: use body symbols only.
4. From what you have learnt from the chapter on Meditation and the section on Worship in this chapter, compose a Mahayana prayer for the protection of this planet.
5. There is no particular Mahayana Buddhist ceremony after someone's death. From what you know about Buddhist (especially Mahayana) beliefs about life and death, devise a Mahayana funeral service. Remember, it is a celebration of life. Think carefully about symbols and offerings, and justify them.
6. Find out if there are any Mahayana groups in your area. Interview members from different groups and compare the differences and similarities.

9

Tibetan Buddhism

- Tantric Buddhism
- Images
- Visualisation
- Gurus

- Worship
- Shrines and Chortens
- Monks
- Death and Rebirth

The land of Tibet is, for the most part, over 16,000 feet above sea level. It consists of huge open spaces surrounded by towering mountains. The air is thin and the wildlife scarce. It would be hard to live in such a place and not think about the ultimate questions of life and death.

For over a thousand years a particularly rich and colourful form of Vajrayana Buddhism has been practised in Tibet and the surrounding countries. It is a form of Buddhism which involves the emotions as well as the mind. In contrast to the simplicity of some other forms, its worship involves chanting and hand movements, richly decorated robes and elaborate images.

For centuries it was little known beyond the Himalayas, cut off from outside influences, now it has spread worldwide.

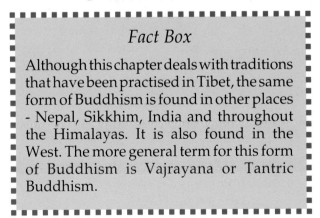

Fact Box

Although this chapter deals with traditions that have been practised in Tibet, the same form of Buddhism is found in other places - Nepal, Sikkhim, India and throughout the Himalayas. It is also found in the West. The more general term for this form of Buddhism is Vajrayana or Tantric Buddhism.

Tibetan worship and images may be more elaborate than those of other branches of Buddhism, but the essence of Buddhism is the same. Like all other Buddhists, Tibetans go to refuge to the Buddha, the Dharma and the Sangha. Guided by their teachers, and allowing their imaginations to enter into their rituals and images, they seek enlightenment - to be fully awake to the truth of life; to cultivate stillness, simplicity and contentment; to share happiness.

Tantric Buddhism

As time goes by, religions change and develop, and in India, from about the 4th century CE, new forms of worship included special rituals, actions and chanting. The idea was to help people to use their imagination and their feelings as well as with their rational minds. The name of this new style of religious practice was called Tantra. Tantric ideas and ceremonies are found in Hinduism as well as Buddhism.

A Buddhist 'goes for refuge' to the Buddha (the ideal of enlightenment), the Dharma (the Buddha's teaching) and the Sangha (the company of all those who follow the Buddha). But following the Buddhist path is not easy - people who want to be Buddhist, often find that there are parts of themselves that are very un-Buddhist - anger, greed, fear, or other deep emotions - and studying the Dharma does not in itself always remove these negative emotions. For that to happen, there has to be some way of getting in touch with feelings, bringing them into the open, and then working to change all their negative energy into positive energy. So, for example, a person who is often angry is using up a great deal of energy in that anger - energy that could be channelled into wisdom, or into positive action.

Tantric Buddhism is the attempt to let Buddhism work on these deeper emotions. It consists of sounds (mantras), hand gestures (mudras) and various rituals, as well as visualisations - in which a person imagines that he or she is actually a Buddha during a period of meditation.

When Buddhism arrived in Tibet in about 700CE, it was already about 1,200 years old. By that time, it included tantric practices. Therefore, the form of Buddhism that took root in Tibet was Tantric. Eventually, Buddhism died out in India, so the Indian tantra disappeared. So this style of Buddhism was preserved in Tibet and neighbouring countries - just as Theravada Buddhism had already spread out and was being preserved in South East Asia, and Mahayana Buddhism further north in China.

Remember: Theravada, Mahayana and Vajrayana (or Tibetan) Buddhism are not three different religions. Each developed out of the earlier forms. Mahayana Buddhism kept the earlier teachings of the Theravada, but added a new dimension to it. Similarly, Vajrayana Buddhism includes things like the 'three refuges' or the 'five precepts' that come from the earliest Buddhist tradition, but adds new things as well.

Question

- The Vajrayana is one of the three 'Yanas'. YANA is a Sanskrit word made up of two parts. 'Ya' can be translated as 'go' and 'na' as 'the means'.

Look up the three yanas on page 38. Then write down a definition of 'yana' in your own words and say why it is a useful word to use in describing the forms of Buddhism.

Distinctive ideas and teachings

These are some of the distinctive features of this kind of Buddhism that we shall be looking at in this chapter:

- Tantric ritual
- Mudras
- Mantras
- The Vajra
- Visualisations
- Prayer wheels and flags
- Lamas (religious teachers)

Question

- How important is it to involve feelings and imagination in religion? Give examples of when you have understood something better through using your imagination, or where you have got to know someone better because of your feelings towards him or her.

Images

As in the Mahayana, Tibetan Buddhism uses many images of Buddhas and Bodhisattvas. Each expresses some particular aspect of enlightenment. Here are some of them:

Avalokitesvara

Avalokitesvara (or Chenrezig, as he is known in Tibet) is the most popular Bodhisattva in Tibetan Buddhism. He represents compassion. He is sometimes shown with one leg up in the position of meditation and the other stepping down towards the world. This shows that he is not remote, but steps down into the world of suffering. Other images of him show him with 1,000 arms. This means that he is there in every situation - each hand ready to help.

A 'thousand armed' Avalokitesvara

Remember: In Tibetan Buddhism, images of Avalokitesvara are male, but 'he' is also found as a female 'Kwan-shih-yin' in Chinese and as Kannon in Japanese Buddhism (see page 98).

(see page 98)

Discuss

• Sometimes Buddhists may describe themselves as being 'hands' of Avalokiteshvara. What do you think this might mean? What would you expect them to do if they think of themselves in this way?

Tara

She also expresses compassion. Some people find that it is easier to relate to a female rather than a male image. Tara is sometimes shown as green in colour; sometimes she is white.

White Tara. Look at her eyes: what is unusual about them?

Questions

• Why do you think some Buddhists find it particularly helpful to have a female image to express the idea of compassion?

• White Tara is shown with extra eyes in her hands, feet and forehead. What do you think these represent?

Vajrapani (wrathful)

Vajrapani expresses energy in persuit of the good. He tramples underfoot all obstacles to enlightenment. He shows great determination.

Visualisation

Be what you want to become!

Those who practise Tantric Buddhism use the same hand movements as their Buddha images. Also, when visualising their Buddhas, they may see themselves as the Buddha. The idea is to enter into what it would be like to be enlightened, to be a Buddha.

Discuss

• Imagine you are enlightened. What do you feel? What do you see? How will you respond to other people?

The aim is to let the mind and the imagination respond to the idea of enlightenment in a very personal way.

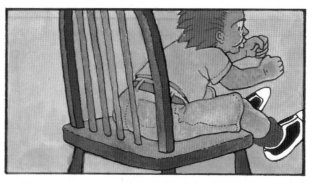

Watch a small child pretend to be driving a car. He or she will hold an imaginary steering wheel and make the noise of the engine. It is pretend, but it also gives the child the happiness and excitement of the real thing. Buddhists follow the same principle - they prepare their minds for enlightenment by acting out what enlightenment would be like.

Fact Box

Details of Tantric rituals or visualisations. are usually kept secret and only revealed to those whom their teacher thinks will benefit from them. Selecting the right practice is very important if a person is to benefit from it. (e.g. a quiet, shy person may need to develop confidence and energy, an angry and insensitive one will need compassion and mindfulness - the wise teacher will choose suitable practices for each of them.)

Activities

Key Elements

1 Which two Bodhisattvas represent compassion?
2 Why do Tantric Buddhists 'act out' enlightenment?

Think About It

3 Why is important to choose the right ritual or visualisation? What might happen if you get the wrong one?

Gurus

As well as Buddhas and Bodhisattvas, Tibetan shrines often have images of famous Buddhist teachers of the past. A teacher is known as a guru, and Tibetan Buddhists feel that the guru represents Buddha to someone here and now. Some of the best known gurus are Padmasambhava, Milarepa and Tsong-ka-pa.

In Tantric Buddhism, a person is given initiation by a guru. This means that he or she receives, with the help of the guru, the energy and insight needed for progress. It is like a seed - the guru gives it, but the disciple needs to take care of it and make it grow. Handing on traditions in this way is important - and Tibetan Buddhists speak of a lineage: a chain of gurus and disciples going back to the great teachers of the past. A disciple who has cultivated the seed can become a guru, and implant that seed in others. Hopefully, the disciple will have learned everything that his master has to offer, and will then add his own experience - possibly becoming an even greater master himself in time.

Padmasambhava is regarded by Tibetan Buddhists as the most important guru. He was the teacher who brought Tantric Buddhism to Tibet from India. He is therefore seen as the one who can interpret the Buddha's teaching so that people can experience it here and now - and for Tibetan Buddhists he is therefore the next most important person after the Buddha himself.

Activities

Key Elements

1 What does Guru mean?
2 Why is Padmasambhava held in special respect by Tibetan Buddhists?

Think About It

3 Explain in your own words why Tibetan Buddhists see it as important to have a teacher.

Activity
BE CAREFUL WHO SEES THIS!
List the subjects you are studying and the teachers who teach them. Which teachers do you like best? (Marks out of 5.) Which subjects do you like best? (Marks out of 5.) How do the marks match up? In what ways do your feelings about your teachers affect your performance in subjects? What qualities do you think a good teacher should have? What about a Tantric Guru?

Milarepa

As a young man, Milarepa practised black magic and killed off some members of his own family. Later he changed complety and became a Buddhist guru. All the energy that had been used destructively was channelled into doing good - but only after a great deal of effort in order to break his selfish and destructive impulses.
By tradition Milarepa lived in a cave throughout the cold Himalayan winters, but he did not need to wear many clothes for he used a special form of mediation that generates body heat. He is believed to have composed and sung many beautiful songs.
Living in great simplicity, he gathered around him a group of followers.

Worship

People make offerings before images of Buddhas and Bodhisattvas, just as in other branches of Buddhism. They may also chant mantras - phrases with a special meaning, but which may have words that do not make literal sense. Sometimes Buddhists make hand movements (called mudras) which express different aspects of enlightenment. They also express their religious ideas through objects, like the vajra and the stupa. We shall examine the meaning of some of these in a moment.

Worship in a Tibetan shrine is rich in colour and sound. Horns may be blown, giving long, deep notes. There may be chanting of mantras over and over. The robes are richly coloured. There may be many candles, in front of the images and around the shrine room. There may be incense burning.

Young monks perform the various rituals and gestures involved in tantric Buddhism. Notice the vajras, bells, horns and offerings of money.

Vajras

The Vajra is an important symbol for Tantric Buddhism. The word vajra means two things:
1   diamond - a hard jewel, which can cut anything else, but cannot itself be cut.
2   thunderbolt - a symbol of power.

It is like a weapon which will always destroy the enemy, always return to the hand of the person who uses it, and cannot be stopped from achieving what is needed. The vajra therefore represents the determination to cut through illusion and to achieve enlightenment.

A vajra and a bell with a vajra handle.
In the centre of the vajra there is a sphere - its perfect and complete shape represents the whole of reality. Out of that sphere come two lotus flowers, one growing upwards the other downwards. The lotus represents growth, and the two of them show that there are two ways of interpreting and responding to reality, one positive, the other negative. From each of those flowers there are five spokes - one in the centre and four at each of the compass points.

There are five special Buddhas, each of which has a particular wisdom associated with him. The five spokes at the top of the vajra represent these. The five spokes at the bottom represent the five elements, the five skandhas (see page 26) and also five poisons (infatuation, hatred, conceit, passion and envy).

You have poisons at one end and wisdoms at the other - so the vajra is a symbol of the determination to transform all of life into something positive. The poisons are not ignored, nor does a person pretend they do not exist, but their energy is converted into something more creative and positive.

Mudras

Gestures are important. You can 'feel' what a gesture means, rather than just understand it.

Tantric Buddhism uses gestures in two ways. They are used in Tantric ritual (in which case the person makes the gesture in the course of worship) and are found on images of Buddhas and Bodhisattvas (in which case they help express what that particular image stands for).

Here are the most important mudras. Each of them is associated with a particular Buddha image, and with a particular quality of wisdom that the Buddha represents.

Earth Touching

Buddhists believe that Buddha, just before he became enlightened, called on the Earth to bear witness to what was happening. It is a gesture that accepts everything just as it is - it 'touches the earth', starts from the 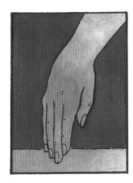 reality of things here and now. It may be used at the beginning of meditation to 'root' the meditator, to start from a person's present situation in the world. 'I feel rooted here, I feel good and solid, this is me!' - that's the sort of feeling that the Earth Touching mudra can evoke.

This mudra is associated with a particular kind of wisdom, the wisdom of the mirror. This is like holding up a mirror, so that a person can take a good look at himself or herself.

Dana-mudra

Dana means giving - the quality of generosity. It is being open handed - offering things to other people. That is what the outward-turned hand expresses. It represents the Wisdom of Equality - treating everybody in 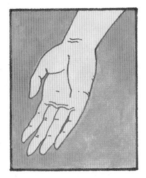 the same way, being as generous to others as you would be to yourself.

Dhyana-mudra

This mudra expresses meditation. It is perfectly balanced and relaxed. The palms of the hands are upturned, being receptive and open to all the eternal qualities. Meditation is a central part of the Buddhist life - 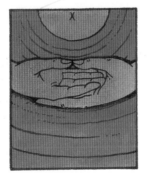 because without meditation, Buddhists feel that they would not be able to develop, or allow the Buddhist teachings to become their natural way to think, feel and act.

The Fearless mudra

A hand raised can be a greeting or a blessing. You can use it to stop traffic. It can show determination and fearlessness. This mudra express the idea of a determined wisdom that overcomes all obstacles.

Dharma-chakra mudra

The part of the body across the chest is often called the 'heart centre' - it is where people often experience their emotions. This mudra is the turning of the wheel of the Dharma (teaching) - putting the Buddhist dharma into operation, but doing it close to the heart. The two hands around the wheel have the right hand turned outwards and the left hand inwards. 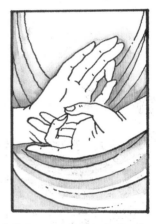 This shows that the Buddhist teaching is both something to apply out in the world, and also something to use to transform the inner self.

Mantras

Buddhists sometimes chant phrases over and over again. These are Mantras - sound symbols which may not have a literal meaning. Some are just words that play on the name of a Buddha or Bodhisattva.

Although the mantra may not have a logical meaning, it represents important feelings. To use a mantra properly, you need to know what it stands for. Then, as you chant it, the feelings and the mantra gradually go together, so that whenever you think of the mantra, you find the feelings start to flow.

Some of the syllables used in mantras are called 'seed syllables' - for just as a seed contains everything that is found in the plant that grows from it, so these syllables contain the whole of the Buddhist path. Three important seed syllables are OM, AH and HUM.

The syllable OM is a very ancient religious symbol. It stands for reality itself - for the goal of the spiritual path. It also includes the idea of opening up to freedom, and is said to describe the idea that the infinite can be found within each individual.

The syllable AH represents communication, and is associated with the throat.

Each part of the seed syllable HUM (which is pronounced 'hoong') represents the wisdom of one of the five Buddhas (see page 110). When a person looks at the symbol written out, or chants it, he or she is reminded of the whole of the Buddhist path.

These three seed syllables are often used at the beginning of Buddhist worship. Standing before a Buddha image, the worshipper puts his or her hands together at the top of the head and says OM, then brings them down to the throat and says AH, and finally down to the heart centre and says HUM. It is a dedication to the Buddha of Body, Speech and Mind. Body is represented by the head, opening out to the universe, and mind is located in the heart - the place where you develop wisdom.

 OM MANI PADME HUM is the mantra of Avalokitesvara. It expresses his compassion for every living thing. Each syllable in this mantra has many meanings. Two of them have already been explained. This is how it is written:

OM   (all of reality / the spiritual path)
MANI   jewel or treasure
PADME lotus (symbol of spiritual growth)
HUM   (wisdom in the heart)
Together they show the idea that the precious jewel of enlightenment is to be found within individuals, in their spiritual development.

Mantras are written out on paper and tucked into prayer wheels. Small prayer wheels are carried in the hand.

... larger ones are fixed, and people turn them with their hands as they pass them.

Tibetan Buddhists believe that the truth represented by OM MANI PADME HUM is there all the time and in everything. Turning a prayer wheel is a reminder of that.

Mantras and seed syllables may also be written or painted on flags and banners. They are not just for decoration, but a reminder of Buddhist teaching.

Questions

• Chanting, candles, images, tankhas (wall hangings) and elaborate costumes are all part of the Tibetan style of Buddhist worship. Do you think these things help a person to be a follower of the Buddha? Give your reasons.

• In Buddhist worship (puja) people sometimes prostrate themselves on the ground (see the photo on page 95). They may bow and make offerings to an image. They may light candles, burn incense and offer flowers. In what ways do people in the West show respect?

• Tibetan shrines are often very colourful, with decorations illustrating features of the Buddhist teaching. How important do you think it is to create an atmosphere for worship? In what ways might you prepare a room for a party? How might you create 'atmosphere'?

Activities

Key Elements

1 What does Vajra mean?
2 What do the following mudras represent? Earth touching, Dana, Dhyana, Fearless, Dharma-chakra.
3 What is the best known Tibetan mantra?

Think About It

4 'The wisdom of the Buddhas and the five poisons come out of the same reality'. Think of situations where good has come out of evil.
6 How do we use hand gestures to express a) come here; b) Well done; c) I'm angry with you; d) I'm your friend?
7 Do sounds need to have a literal meaning? What is the meaning of screaming, or crying, or laughing? What about music?

Shrines and Chortens

The shrine rooms used by Tibetan Buddhists tend to be richly decorated, often with wall hangings (called thankas) of the many Buddhas and Bodhisattvas.

These images are like visual aids - they are ways of expressing what Buddhism is about, and also ways to help people to meditate.

Tibetan Buddhists have stupas, just as in the earlier forms of Buddhism. They are called Chortens. Traditionally, these contain the remains of the Buddha, one of his enlightened followers, or great Buddhist teachers of the past. But they are not mere monuments - as with most things in the Buddhist world, they are visual aids, and the clue to one of their meanings for Tibetan Buddhists is given in the fact that it has eyes.

This decorated chorten in Nepal has a special, symbolic meaning - and the clue is in the eyes!

Elements of the Stupa.

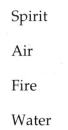

Spirit

Air

Fire

Water

Earth

Stupas are made up five parts which represent various elements, starting with the most solid - earth - at the base and going up to pure spirit (or space) at the top. In this way the stupa represents the whole of reality.

But these elements in a stupa can also stand for parts of a human being. These are not things that you would find physically in the body. (They do not appear in books on anatomy!) Rather, they express where people tend to experience their thoughts and feelings:

- The cube and sphere represent the lower parts of the body, the place where many deep feelings and needs are felt.
- The red cone represents the heart centre, the place from which you experience emotions and make choices (feelings of great happiness or sadness may be experienced in the chest).
- The green inverted hemisphere represents the throat, and speech.

Discuss

Have you ever described someone as wooden or earthy? Or fluid in his or her ideas? Or fiery? Or free as the air? What might a stupa composed of the five elements say about the Buddhist path?

- The multi-coloured droplet on the top represents the crown of the head and the ideas of enlightenment.

Parts of the human body, represented by the elements in the stupa.

So the stupa (or chorten) represents the idea of enlightenment.

At the base of the fire element, chortens have a box, called a harmika. This may contain the remains of the person in whose memory the stupa is built, but it also represents an altar where offerings would be put on a sacred fire. Although the whole stupa represents the Buddha, the harmika represents the point of choice, where a person takes the step towards enlightenment. It has to do with the heart, and to do with making offerings. It has eyes; it watches you!

Traditionally, each side of the stupa represents a moment in the life of Gautama. You find that some stupas have images to express this.

East - birth
South - enlightenment
West - teaching
North - death (parinirvana)

Buddhists walk round a stupa in a clockwise direction - that way they follow the life of the Buddha from birth to death.

Activities

Key Elements

1 What is a Tibetan stupa called?
2 What are the Five Elements?

Think About It

3 Why do you think Buddhists use images to help them understand their religion? Do you think an image is more or less helpful than a written description of something? Give your reasons.
4 The Five Elements used to be thought to be the basic components of life, the foundations of everything. Why these five, do you think?
5 Why do you think the chorten has eyes? What do they suggest to you?
6 Events from the Buddhas life are represented on the sides of stupas. Why is his birth shown on the East?

A note: Religion and Culture

Tibetan Buddhism may seem very different from the simple Buddhism of the Theravada tradition. It is almost as if the Tibetans practise a different religion; the moral principles are the same, but the forms of worship are different.

Some people argue that these depend on the culture of the people and are not an essential part of the religion itself. Tibetan society was suited to this Tantric form of Buddhism.

Using 'skilful means' (knowing the right thing to do in any situation) a teacher of the Dharma tries to find the best way to present an idea, so that his hearers can understand it. So Buddhism has adapted itself for different cultures. We should not to ask 'Which is the real Buddhism?', it depends on the people.

The Dharma is like a raft that is used to cross a river and is then thrown away. What matters is that people find this particular raft useful. It does not have to be the same for everybody.

Monks

Until the middle of the 20th century the religious life of Tibet was dominated by huge monasteries. It was estimated that one in three of all men became monks and up to one fifth of the entire population lived in monasteries. The capital city, Lhasa, had a population of only 20,000, but around it were monasteries with another 20,000 monks living in them.

There are different sects within the Tibetan monastic sangha. The oldest of these is the Nyingmapa (Red Hats), names after their ceremonial headgear. The Gelugpa (Yellow Hats), a reformed group set up in the 14th century, is the largest sect today.

Young boys may become monks. They take temporary vows and are educated in the monastery. As well as reading, writing and maths, they also study Tibetan Buddhist philosophy and scriptures. Most Tibetan men have therefore had at least some experience of monastic life

Fully ordained monks are called Gelongs, and senior teachers are known as Lamas. Some Lamas are monks, but others are married and have a family life alongside their teaching.

Tibetan monks follow many of the same traditions as those of other Branches of Buddhism, but they do not go out of their monasteries (which are called lamaseries) to receive offerings from lay people.

There is a tradition of serious study among Tibetan monks. They have to learn how to defend an argument point by point, and train by taking part in debates.

The Dalai Lama

The Dalai Lama is head of the Gelugpa order of monks and is seen as the spiritual leader of the Tibetan people. The Chinese invaded Tibet in 1950 and by 1951 had taken the capital, Lhasa. For some time, the Dalai Lama remained in the country, but in 1959 there was a uprising against the Chinese, and he and many of his followers fled across the border into Northern India, where he settled in a place called Dharamsala.

Tibetan monks wear deep red robes (Theravadin monks wear saffron yellow; Far Eastern monks wear black).

Fact Box

Dalai means 'sea' - representing that which is deep and measureless
Lama means 'teacher'
So the title ***Dalai Lama*** means the 'deep one', or the 'profound teacher'.
Each Dalai Lama is thought to be the reincarnation (tulku, see page 117) of the previous Dalai Lama. He is also thought to be the living form of Avalokitesvara, the Bodhisattva of Compassion. The Dalai Lama is sometimes referred to as the 'god-king of Tibet', but this is not correct.

From there he has worked to help the people of his country, and to make their troubles known to the rest of the world.

At first, after the rebellion, the Chinese tried to eradicate the Buddhist religion. Many of the great monasteries were destroyed and monks were killed. Since then, from time to time, the situation has become easier, and there have been discussions about the possibility that the Dalai Lama might return one day. In 1994, however, in a further attempt to remove signs of his influence, the Chinese ordered that all photographs and paintings of the Dalai Lama should be removed from homes. Previously it had been common for Tibetans to have a photo of the Dalai Lama, which served as a focus for their worship and reminded them of their Buddhist history and traditions.

Death and Rebirth

Like most Eastern religions, Buddhism has the idea of 'again becoming' (or rebirth). After death, the karma that a person has developed in this life (see pages 26 and 27) is believed to carry on having its effects. This does not mean that the actual person moves on into another life (Buddhism does not think of a person as having a fixed 'soul') but that a new life will arise in a way that is influenced by the life that is ending.

Most people have no idea what those long-term effects of their karma will be. But in the case of religious teachers (lamas), Tibetan Buddhists believe that they can choose the next life that they will influence. A child that is believed to be the reincarnation of a lama is called a Tulku.

When a senior lama dies, the monks seek out the child who is thought to be the reincarnation of their dead teacher, and arrange tests to see if a particular child is the tulku. Sometimes the child is asked to select personal belongings from the dead lama from among a pile of similar ones.

Some people think that you can remember something of past lives. In this way a young child, although not consious of it, may have some sense of having been the old lama.

This is an account of two events that led some people to think that a child called Osel was a reincarnate lama:

> Osel was born in Spain to Buddhist parents. His name means 'clear light'. His mother had a dream about Lama Yeshe, who had died in America in 1984. She sensed that the lama was telling her not to grieve for him. At that time, while she was thinking about Lama Yeshe, she found that she was pregnant. One year after Osel was born, a lama came to see him and laid out five sets of prayer beads. The child looked at them and chose a very plain set - which had belonged to Lama Yeshe, - rather than the more brightly brightly coloured ones that a child might have been expected to choose. Osel was later taken to see the Dalai Lama in India. He was crying when he arrived at the room where he was to meet the Dalai Lama, but suddenly he became quiet. He toddled over to a table on which there were some gifts and picked up a white flower
> that was to have been given to him. then he went over to the Dalai Lama and tapped him on the forehead with it!

These things led people to think that Osel was in fact a tulku - the reincarnation of Lama Yeshe.

Question

- What do you think about the events described here? Do they prove anything? What do they suggest to you about the boy?

Death

The Tibetan Book of the Dead is advice given to someone who is dying. It tells him or her not to worry, but explains the various stages through which he or she will go before taking on another life. The time in between one life and the next is called the Bardo - traditionally it may last for just a moment, or for as long as 49 days. Tibetan Buddhists believe that as you enter the Bardo, you are given various choices. What you choose depends on how you have lived your life, but it also determines what sort of life you will influence in the future. In this way, your own deeds and attitudes lead you to choose another life.

The Tibetan Book of the Dead reads rather like a science fantasy adventure. You see various coloured lights and are drawn towards one of them, this determines the realm into which you are to be born. Finally, if you are to be born a human, you see couples making love, and feel attracted towards one of them. In this way, you choose your next parents!

Not every Buddhist would say that all the details in the Tibetan Book of the Dead are to be taken literally - because it is something about which people cannot have direct knowledge (unless you could manage to remember and understand it, once you had grown up in your next life). But it is an important book for showing the values by which Buddhists live, and the way in which, as someone approaches death, his or her life can be put into perspective.

Activities

Key Elements

1 What is the capital of Tibet?
2 What does Lama mean?
3 What does Dalai mean?
4 Outline the Buddhist view of rebirth in your own words.
5 What is a Tulku?
6 What is the Tibetan Book of the Dead about?

Think About It

7 Why would the Chinese invaders want pictures of the Dalai Lama removed?
8 When asked if he hated the Chinese soldiers, the Dalai Lama said he did not. In fact, he wanted to help them by transferring merit to them. Do you believe him? Is it really possible to love your enemies?
9 How would a Buddhist answer the question. "Why can't you remember your previous lives?"
10 Why are Buddhists not concerned about trying to find out details of previous lives?
11 Explain what a Buddhist would mean by saying that you choose the circumstances of your next birth by the actions you make in this life?
12 Have you ever had the experience of feeling that you have been somewhere before, or that a strange place is actually familiar to you? Do you think these experiences mean that a person may 'become again' in different lives? What other explanations might be given for them?

Assignments

1 Look at the images from three different branches of the Buddhist religion. List their main features, and then say which of them you prefer and why.
2 Design a poster showing the distinctive features of Tibetan Buddhism.
3 Using one of the Five Poisons as a theme (infatuation, hatred, conceit, passion, envy), write a story of how a negative situation can be tranformed into a positive one.
4 Illustrate the mudras carefully and make a class display.
5 Find out about the Chinese invasion of Tibet and its impact on the people there. (Contact Amnesty International for more information about this.)
6 Research the life of the Dalai Lama and write a short biography.
7 Some Tibetan monks and nuns have been imprisoned and tortured. Write a letter to encourage and inspire a monk or nun from a Buddhist point of view.
8 Watch the film "The Little Buddha" and write a review of it.

10

Buddhism in the West

- Adapting and Growing
- Some Buddhist Groups in Britain

Adapting and Growing

We have seen how Buddhism started in Northern India and spread out to the countries of South East Asia, Nepal, Tibet and the Far East. As it spread, it adapted itself to meet the needs of the people it encountered.

A skilful teacher knows how to adapt his teaching to the needs of his hearers. Buddhist teachers have always done this and as Buddhism becomes established in the West it will gradually develop forms that are particularly Western.

Although some people in the West had heard about Buddhism, and Christian missionaries had gone to the East to try to convert Buddhists, it was not until the 19th century that western scholars started to take an interest in Buddhist scriptures. In fact, the term *Buddhism* was first used at that time to describe the religion of those who followed the Dharma.

By the end of the 19th century there developed a rather romantic idea of the Orient as a magical, spiritual place, a place of secrets and profound mysteries. Museums displayed Eastern art, including Buddhist images. It became fashionable to have oriental decorations, and the wealthy collected oriental art. Most people thought about Buddhism as something exotic and distant, unrelated to their own lives.

Although individual Buddhists had lived in the West, it was not until the second half of the 20th century that people started to think of Buddhism as a religion by which Western people might live and it was only then that

Buddhist communities were established in the West.

There were several reasons for the increase in interest in Buddhism:

- People find it easier to move about the world today; there are many Thais, Burmese, Japanese, Tibetans and Chinese living in the West. They continue to practise their religion following the traditions they were used to in their countries of origin and have built shrines here in the same style as those in the East.
- Sometimes even war can spread an interest in Buddhism. After World War II American forces were stationed in Japan; later they were involved in the war in Korea. This brought Americans into contact with Buddhists from those countries.

Fact Box

The different forms of Buddhism are often associated with the parts of the world in which they developed - but they are practised all over the world.

So, you can practise Tibetan Buddhism without going to Tibet or Nepal, you can follow Zen without ever having been to Japan.

Each form of Buddhism has features which come from the culture in which it developed, but these are less important that the Dharma itself.

- During the Vietnam War, many American soldiers became interested in Buddhism, which they came across for the first time. At the end of the war, some of them wanted to continue to find more about it. Others married girls from Vietnam or Thailand and took them back to the United States. There were also refugees from the war who moved to the United States, bringing their religion with them. This accounted for much of the growth of Buddhism in America from the 1970s
- In the 1960s, Buddhist teachers started to come to the West. In particular, after the Chinese invasion of Tibet in 1959, Tibetan Lamas started teaching outside their own country, many coming to the United States and to Europe.

Establishing Communities

Some forms of Buddhism in the West are the same as those found in the East, as those who have come from traditionally Buddhist countries, but have now settled in the West, continue their traditional form of worship. These communities have been joined by those Westerners who also want to practise in that way. So you have Theravadin, Zen, Tibetan, Nichiren and other Buddhist communities, with members from both East and West.

There are also new forms of Buddhism which have developed in the West, and which are specially suited to Westerners. The most widespread of these is the Friends of the Western Buddhist Order.

Some Buddhist Groups in Britain

There are many Buddhists in the USA and in the rest of Europe, but if you visited a Tibetan, Zen or FWBO centre in California, France, or Germany it would not be significantly different from a centre in Britain, so we shall now look at Buddhists in Britain.

There are more than 200 Buddhist centres and organisations in Britain. The numbers of people practising in them are divided very approximately as follows:

30%	Theravada
20%	Tibetan
15%	Zen
15%	Friends of the Western Buddhist Order
20%	Nichiren and others

Zen

There are many Zen groups in Britain and elsewhere in the West. Zen became popular first in the 1950s as a form of mental training which could be adopted by Westerners who might not be ready for the whole range of Buddhist teachings.

Most Western groups follow a tradition called

Soto Zen. One such organisation is the Order of Buddhist Contemplatives, which has its European Centre at Throssel Hole Priory in Northumberland, and now runs 32 monasteries.

Nipponzan Myohoji

Formed in Japan with a special concern to promote world peace, this Nichiren Buddhist group has built Peace Pagodas throughout the world, including those in London and Milton Keynes.

Monks from this movement take part in demonstrations, work alongside other groups promoting peace, and have daily rituals in which they chant for peace.

The Peace Pagoda in Batersea Park, London.

Theravada

The Theravada tradition in Britain has been led by Westerners who have gone east to train as monks and then returned to establish monastic centres. In 1926, Anagarika Dharmapala founded a branch of the Maha Bodhi Society in London, which survived until shortly after the start of the World War II. The Buddhist Lodge of the Theosophical Society under the leadership of Christmas Humphreys became The Buddhist Society in 1943. It was the main focus for Buddhism in Britain until other groups started to be established in the 1960s.

Things were not always easy for the new communities. Some members of the Buddhist Society formed the English Sangha Trust hoping to establish an ordained monastic sangha in Britain. In 1954 an English Buddhist who had trained as a monk in Thailand was ordained and given the name Kapilavaddho. He returned to England to work with the English Sangha Trust. At one time there were up to four monks, but the last of them returned to Thailand in 1961. Two other monks tried to continue a monastic life at the Hampstead vihara, the base for the Trust's work, and in 1967 Kapilavaddho returned to continue running it for some time. But then is was empty of monks until 1977.

The Thai forest tradition

Ajahn Chah was born in 1918, and entered the monastic life at the age of 21. He chose to live as a 'forest monk' - giving much of his time to meditation - rather than working in one of the cities, where he would have had many administrative and practical duties. He lived for some time wandering in the forests of Thailand and meditating. In 1954 he settled back near his home, and started to attract other people who wanted to follow his way of life. Many Westerners came to join him in Thailand, including a young American who arrived in 1967, who was later to be ordained as Ajahn Sumedho.

Sumedho spent ten years living in the forest tradition Ajahn Chah, and became the first abbot of a monastery for training Westerners. In 1977 he was invited to establish a monastic community in England. He started off at the vihara in Hampstead.

One day, Ajahn Sumedho attracted the attention of a jogger on Hampstead Heath, who, hearing about the community, gave them a wood in Sussex to care for. The following year, the Trust sold the Hampstead house and bought one near the wood - which became the Chithurst monastery. It is now used as a place where new monks are trained before they go to work at Amaravati, the main centre in Hertfordshire.

The monastery at Amaravati welcomes visitors. The monks and nuns lead meditation classes and give talks, as well as following their own studies and other work. Visitors, like the members of the community, are expected to get up early for meditation and puja, and to have only one main meal, just before midday. (The timetable for a typical day at Amaravati is given on page 83.)

The monastery depends on gifts in order to keep going. It accepts these, and in return provides a place of peace, of meditation, and a place where people can go to learn to cultivate calm and contentment for themselves.

Question and Discussion
- From what you know of Theravada Buddhism, what feature of the daily life of a monk in the East would you not expect to find in the West? (Clue: Where do they go?)
- What do you think the monks should do about this?

Fact Box
The monks at Chithurst (Cittaviveka) and Amaravati are Western. There are many other monks in Britain who come from traditional Buddhist countries and help Buddhists from those countries who have settled in Britain. For example, in London there is a Burmese Vihara, a Thai temple in Wimbledon and the London Buddhist Vihara which follows the Buddhist traditions of Sri Lanka.

SGI

Nichiren was a Japanese Buddhist priest who lived in the 13th century. He took the Lotus Sutra as the basis of his teaching, and encouraged his followers to chant as a form of mental training.

The mantra used by Nichiren Buddhists is *Nam-myoho-renge-kyo.* We saw on page 48 that 'Myoho-renge-kyo' is the title of the Lotus Sutra in classical Japanese, and that 'Nam-myoho-renge-kyo' means, 'I devote myself to the Mystic Law of the Dharma and karma for eternity.'

Nichiren Buddhists believe that chanting this mantra daily, along with passages from the Lotus Sutra, draws out a person's potential for Buddhahood and can also lead to positive success in life. They believe that the chanting puts them in touch with the fundamental rhythm of the universe and that this will have a positive effect on every area of a person's life, including their work and their relationships.

The main organisation for Nichiren Buddhists in Britain is called SGI-UK: the United Kingdom branch of Sokka Gakkai International. Soka Gakkai means 'Society for the Creation of Value' and is an organization which began in Japan before the Second World War. It has now spread to well over a hundred countries throughout the world, and is the largest Buddhist group in Japan. Its UK headquarters are at Taplow Court in Berkshire.

Sokka Gakkai is a lay organisation, which means that it does not follow the leadership of the Nichiren priests in Japan. Its stated aims are to create world peace through activities based on culture and education.

This form of Buddhism has attracted some well-known names in the West, including actors and actresses, pop and rock stars and fashion designers. Taking up Buddhism in order to become more creative and successful is appealing, but, of course, a Buddhist would say that you have to do it for the right reasons.

Tibetan

There are many Tibetan centres in Europe and America. The first to be established in Britain was called Samye Ling. This monastery and retreat centre is set in the Scottish borders, and monks from Samye Ling have set up the Holy Island project, hoping that the ancient Western religious centre on Holy Island can be developed as a place of retreat for people of all faiths.

Another Important centre is the Manjushri Institute in Cumberland. This is an independent Tibetan centre particularly concerned to adapt Tibetan Buddhism for people in the West.

Retreats

Some Tibetans go into retreat for long periods. In 1993, a group of 35 Buddhists emerged from the Samye Ling Tibetan monastery in Eskdalemuir in the Scottish borders, after four years. Only nine people had dropped out during the four years - one of them an elderly Tibetan monk, who later died of cancer. They spent much of their time in meditation and in study. Although generally on their own, they did meet one another for meals. For a period of six months, they stayed in complete silence.

> ### Discuss
>
> A long retreat is a difficult thing for a person to cope with.
> - What do you think you would find most difficult?
> - What might be the advantages of going on retreat?
> - What would you most miss in the outside world?

Some old Tibetan customs would not be welcomed by most people in the West. In Tibet, firewood is scarce and the ground is rocky, so it is not easy to bury or cremate the dead. So bodies were carried to the top of mountains, hacked to pieces and spread round to feed the birds and wild animals. It was a very practical way of disposing of them and it said something important about the human body from a Buddhist perspective, but it would probably be misunderstood in the West. It is important to recognise which cultural features can be adapted for use in the West and which cannot.

FWBO

So far we have looked at forms of Buddhism which have been 'imported' into the West from the East. Many of their features are the same as you would find in their country of origin. But new forms of Buddhism have developed, especially suited to life in the West.

The Friends of the Western Buddhist Order (FWBO) was founded Britain in the 1960s by Dennis Lingwood. He had become interested in Buddhism as a young man living in South London, and become more involved when he was sent to India as a soldier during the Second World War. After the war, he stayed in India and became a Buddhist monk. He was ordained as a Theravadin, but later also studied under Tibetan and Zen teachers. When he was ordained he was given a Buddhist name - Sangharakshita - which means 'one who builds up the Sangha'.

In 1964 he returned to Britain, and for two years he worked at the Hampstead Buddhist Vihara. He came to believe that a new form of Buddhism was needed for people in the West, a form which would use the earlier traditions, but adapt them to the needs of Western people.

He founded the Friends of the Western Buddhist Order in 1967 and the following year ordained the first members of the Western Buddhist Order.

The central feature of the Buddhist life, according to Sangharakshita, is 'going for refuge' (see chapter three), and a person is ordained into the Western Buddhist Order when their effective 'going for refuge' is recognised and accepted by members of the Order. They do not have to take on special monastic vows. The Western Buddhist Order is neither monastic nor lay. The common feature is commitment to the Three Jewels. Those who are ordained are called Dharmachari (male) or Dharmacharini (female), meaning 'Tarers in the Dharma', in other words, those who put the Dharma into practice in their daily lives.

At the same time as getting that title, the person who is ordained gets a new name. It may be in Pali or Sanskrit, and it generally reflects a quality that the person already has or which he or she is encouraged to develop further.

Some order members live together in single-sex communities, others live on their own, with partners or friends, or with wives and families. Sangharakshita emphasises that commitment comes first and lifestyle second. In other words, a person has to make his or her commitment to the Three Jewels, and then the right way for that particular person to live will come about naturally as a result.

Members of the order wear ordinary clothes, but have a special scarf (called a kesa) to show that they have been ordained into the Western Buddhist Order. They wear the kesa when teaching or leading puja.

This Order Member is wearing her kesa. It is decorated with an emblem representing the three Jewels - the Buddha, the Dharma and the Sangha.

The FWBO runs Buddhist Centres and retreat centres. People who attend these and start to practise Buddhism are called 'Friends'. Those who have been involved for some time, and want to support and develop their friendships with Order Members, may become 'Mitras' (*Mitra* is the Sanskrit term for 'friend').

Some Friends, Mitras and Order Members work together in 'team-based Right Livelihood' businesses (see page 73). These provide a good environment within which to earn a living, and also generate money to support the work of the Centres. Unlike communities in traditional Buddhist countries, there are few people to offer financial support, and the movement relies on these businesses and the generosity (dana) of those who take part in its Buddhist activities.

The challenge facing Buddhism in the West today is knowing how to present the Dharma in a way that people can understand and accept, without diluting it to make it fit in with Western ideas and attitudes. To do that will require two great Buddhist qualities - wisdom and compassion.

A shrine in North Wales. The Buddha image may be traditional, but its features are Western, and the cushions scattered in front of it are for a practice of meditation that is just as relevant to people living in the West as in the East.

Activities

Key Elements

1 In which century did Western scholars start to take an interest in the Dharma and its scriptures?
2 When was the term 'Buddhism' first used?
3 What is the name of the main Nichiren organisation in Britain?
4 Who founded the FWBO, and when?

Think About It

5 Using the example of the old Tibetan custom of exposing dead bodies (see page 122), explain in your own words why a Buddhist has to distinguish between things that are part of the Dharma and those that belong to a particular culture or particular circumstances?
6 If you were to be ordained into the Western Buddhist Order, you would be given a new name. Do you think it is a good idea to have a special religious name as well as the one your parents gave you? Give your reasons for and against.
7 If you met a lay Buddhist, you would not know that he or she followed the Dharma from his or her appearance. So how might you recognise a Buddhist? What would he or she be like? What characteristics would you look for? Write a list of the qualities you would expect him or her to have.

Assignment

Looking back through this chapter and then through the book as a whole, write brief answers to the following:
• What features of Buddhism might be most difficult for someone in the West to accept?
• What do you think the West might learn from Buddhism that would benefit it?
• List the changes in a person's life that might come about if he or she became a committed Buddhist.

Glossary

Where Pali and Sanskrit versions of a term are found widely, both are included here, even if only one has been used in the text of this book. Where only one version is given, it indicates that the term is generally found in that language. In other cases, the Pali and Sanskrit words may be the same, or a word may be of Tibetan or Japanese origin.

Abhidhamma (P), Abhidharma (Sk)
'Higher teaching'; Buddhist philosophy

Abhidamma Pitaka (P), Abhidharma Pitaka (Sk) Third section of the Pali canon; systematic and philosophical approach to the Dharma.

Anatta (P), Anatman (Sk) No independent or permanent self.

Anicca (P), Anitya (Sk) All things are impermanent.

Arahat (P), Arhat (Sk) An enlightened disciples (within the Theravada tradition).

Bardo The time between a person's death and rebirth (found in Tbetan Buddhism).

Bhikku (P), Bhikshu (Sk) Buddhist monk.

Bhikkuni (P), Bhikshuni (Sk) Buddhist nun.

Bodhi Tree Title given to the pipal tree under which the Buddha is said to have gained enlightenment.

Bodhisattva (Sk) One who seeks enlightenment for the sake of all living beings; a figure representing an aspect of enlightenment, especially in Mahayana tradition; Gautama prior to his enlightenment.

Brahma Viharas Four states to be cultivated in meditation: loving kindness, compassion, sympathetic joy and evenness of mind.

Buddha One who is fully awake or enlightened.

Butsudan Japanese term for a shrine.

Chorten Tibetan term for a stupa.

Dagoba Sri Lankan term for a stupa.

Dana Generosity.

Dhamma (P), Dharma (Sk) The teaching of the Buddha; ultimate truth; also used to mean 'thing'.

Dukkha Suffering; the failure of ordinary life to give complete satisfaction.

Gelong Tibetan term for a monk.

Gohonzon A scroll used as a focus for chanting by some Nichiren Buddhists.

Jhana (P), Dhyana (Sk) State of mind achieved in meditation.

Juzu Japanese term for a string of beads used to aid meditation.

Kamma (P), Karma (Sk) Morally significant actions which influence one's future.

Karuna Compassion.

Kesa A robe worn by Japanese monks, nuns or priests; also the small ritual scarf worn by members of the Western Buddhist Order.

Kshanti (Sk) Patience.

Koan A question with no logical meaning or answer, used in Zen Buddhism to encourage insight that goes beyond reason.

Lama Teacher (in Tibetan Buddhism).

Magga (P), Marga (Sk) The Middle Way - the path leading away from suffering (Fourth Noble Truth).

Mahayana One of the three Buddhist 'vehicles'. It emphasises the goal of enlightenment for the sake of all living beings.

Mala String of beads used as an aid to mindfulness, especially when reciting mantras.

Mandala Pattern created to represent spiritual reality, often showing five Buddhas; used also of the pattern of one's personal values or the arrangement of Buddhist groups and individuals who practise together.

Mantra A phrase chanted during worship; often without a literal meaning. It represents and evokes a particular aspect of enlightenment.

Metta Loving kindness.

Mudra (Sk) Ritual guesture used in Tibetan worship; hand position on a Buddha image.

Mudita Sympathetic joy

Nibbana (P), Nirvana (Sk) State of peace achieved when the fires of greed, hatred and ignorance are extinguished.

Nirodha The cessation of suffering (Third Noble Truth)

Pagoda Burmese term for a stupa

Paramita (Sk) Perfection.

Parinibbana (P), Parinirvana (Sk) Complete Nirvana; used of the death of the Buddha.

Patimokkha (P), Patimoksha (Sk) Rules for monks and nuns.

Pitaka Literally 'basket', used of the early collections of Buddhist scriptures.

Prajna (Sk) Wisdom.

Punna (P), Punya (Sk) Merit gained through religious or moral activity.

Rupa Form or body; one of the five aspects of the self; also used of Buddha images.

Sakyamuni (P), Shakyamuni (Sk) The historical Buddha.

Samadhi State of deep meditation.

Samatha Meditation practice aimed at bringing about calmness.

Samsara The ordinary, ever-changing world.

Samudaya The arising of suffering (second Noble Truth)

Sangha Fellowship of those who follow the teachings of the Buddha.

Satori Sudden insight (used in Zen Buddhism).

Sila Morality.

Skandha (Sk) Literally 'heap'; a person is made up of 5 skandhas (form, feelings, perceptions, thoughts, consciousness).

Stupa Monument containing the remains of the Buddha or a member of the Sangha.

Sutta Literally 'string', refers to a text giving a teaching.

Tanha (P) Craving; desire springing out of ignorance; the cause of suffering.

Tathagata 'One who has gone beyond'; used of the Buddha.

Thanka A cloth wall-hanging, generally depicting one or more Buddhas.

Thera Theravadin title used for a senior monk.

Theravada 'Way of the Elders'; used of the branch of the Sagha

Tripitaka 'Three Baskets', collections of texts (Vinaya, Sutta and Abhidamma)

Tiratana (P), Triratna (Sk) The Three Jewels - Buddha, Dharma and Sangha.

Tulku A child who is believed to be the reincarnation of a lama.

Upaya Skilful means - knowing the right thing to do in a particular situation.

Vajrayana One of the three Buddhist 'vehicles'. Today it is represented by Tibetan Buddhism.

Vihara 'Resting place'; used of monasteries.

Vinaya The rules for monks and nuns.

Vipassana Meditation leading to insight.

Viriya (P), Virya (Sk) Energy directed to doing good.

Wat A temple (term used particularly in Thailand).

Wesak Festival held in month of same name, remembering the birth, enlightenment and death of the Buddha.

Zazen Sitting meditation in Zen Buddhism.

Zen A form of Mahayana Buddhism based on meditation, developed in Japan.

Zendo Zen meditation hall

Index